T0208718

Don't Tell Me I Can't

Nancy Elizabeth Phillips

WESTBOW°
PRESS
A DIVISION OF THOMAS NELSON
& ZONDERVAN

WestBow Press books may be ordered through booksellers or by contacting:

WestBow Press
A Division of Thomas Nelson & Zondervan
1663 Liberty Drive
Bloomington, IN 47403
www.westbowpress.com
1 (866) 928-1240

Because of the dynamic nature of the Internet, any web addresses or
links contained in this book may have changed since publication and
may no longer be valid. The views expressed in this work are solely those
of the author and do not necessarily reflect the views of the publisher,
and the publisher hereby disclaims any responsibility for them.

Any people depicted in stock imagery provided by Thinkstock are models,
and such images are being used for illustrative purposes only.
Certain stock imagery © Thinkstock.

ISBN: 978-1-4908-4851-8 (sc)
ISBN: 978-1-4908-4858-7 (e)

Library of Congress Control Number: 2014914675

Printed in the United States of America.

WestBow Press rev. date: 12/4/2014

Don't tell me I can't recounts the life, the struggles of depression, and anxiety that the author has had since early childhood and is continuing to experience. The author tells of her innermost feelings on the darkest days when she experienced depression and anxiety. She, also, describes the darkest time when she realizes that she may never see her two children again after the judge hands down the final decision of the divorce.

Disclaimer

All names in this book are fictitious. No names mentioned have had anything to do with anything in this story, but this is a real account of some of the darkest times of depression, anxiety and suicidal thoughts of the author. The places are considered to be in the Midwest section of the United States.

DEDICATION

First of all, I would like to thank my parents for raising me in a Christian based home. My parents had a positive influence on me when it came to going to church and being involved in the youth group. My dad taught youth Sunday school for years. I would like to dedicate this book to my mom who passed away in the summer of 2011. My mom held me when I was having a hard day. She comforted me and said encouraging words when I would be hearing voices or when I was feeling suicidal which were many times. She prayed for me when I could not pray for myself. Mom cried with me when I was having a bad day. She bought my clothes when I needed them because I gained one hundred pounds in six months which meant my mom had to literally buy my clothes every week because of my weight gain so fast. Without my parents and God, I would not be here today.

In addition, to my mom, my dad inspires me to be all that I can be even on my worst days. Dad offers prayers on my behalf and he reminds me of the scripture verse that says, "Take therefor no thought for the morrow: for the morrow shall take thought for the things of itself. Sufficient unto the day is the evil thereof." Mt. 6:34 KJV. My dad always has words of wisdom for me and helps me to think when I cannot think for myself. I would like to say a big, "Thank you." to my dad for editing my book. He helped to make this publishing a reality. When my Mom was alive, she took me to get my nails done every two weeks because I could not afford to get them done by myself. Now, Dad as a Christmas gift pays for me to get my nails done once a month and a pedicure once every three months. Also, I would like to dedicate this book to my two children, Betty and Andrew, whom I love very much, and they love me back. I have changed their names to protect their real identity. They are what keeps me going on bad days and on the days that I am suicidal. If it were not for their love, I would have killed myself a long time ago. I, also, want to dedicate this book to my sister and her husband. My sister has a kind heart and knows what it is like to have a family member, who has a mental illness. I, also, want to dedicate this book to my brother and his wife who want desperately to do what they can to help me. My brother and his wife have gone to see my therapist with me and have completed a program for families who have a loved one who has a mental illness. My friends in my Sunday school classes where I go when I visit my children are next in line. Also, I would like to dedicate this book to my class in my home church, my friends from the YMCA, and my therapy groups. I would, also, like to thank all the staff at the hospitals since I have been in the hospital over 30 times. I would like to thank my doctors over the years as well. In addition to all of these folks, I would like to thank my friends that I've grown up with and new friends from Celebrate Recovery. Next to last, I want to thank my therapists, and finally and most importantly God who has kept me alive when I did not want to be. God is my life preserve. Without Him, I would be lifeless.

I have journals from 1985-1987, 1995 to 1997, and from May 2010 until July 2012. Then, I started again in 2013 and I am currently continuing to journal. In 1998, when I went to get my journals that contain my own private thoughts from our house, they were missing. However, during the divorce hearing, they were used against me to have my children taken from me. Following the court hearing, the judge ordered that Nick, my ex-husband, return the journals to me. I have used them sporadically throughout my book.

I have wanted to write this book for a long time. I actually started writing *Don't Tell Me I Can't* in 2012 and now you can see it in print. In 1997, a nurse and a doctor from one of the hospitals told me that I would never work again nor would I be a Mom to my two children, and I needed to accept it. Since that time I worked twelve years nine of which were full time, and I am a good Mom to my children Betty and Andrew. Thus, came the title *Don't Tell Me I Can't*.

I believe that at this time in my life God wants me to share my testimony and give God the glory for what He has done in my life.

One day I was in a Christian book store and saw an ad saying that if you would like to see your own book on the shelf then, read this pamphlet that said you need 45,000 words. I thought that I could write more than that which I have done.

CHAPTER ONE

My life of anxiety began when I was three years old when I flushed my grandpa's false teeth down the toilet because I thought it was cereal in a Peanut Butter jar. My mom told me that I did not speak for a week because I was so scared of them being mad at me. I still struggle with people being mad at me. My grandpa told my parents that "Those teeth never fit right in the first place." Thanks Grandpa! My grandmother said, "Now, we can get him a new set of dentures."

At that time, my grandparents owned a hotel where my family visited. Some guests would come and live in the hotel for weeks at a time. I have fond memories of riding my big wheel in the hallways. There was a drugstore below the hotel that my grandpa used to take me to buy candy bars. Grandpa was not supposed to eat candy bars because he was a diabetic, but that did not seem to bother him.

There were, also, some of the residents that treated me special. One gave me candy and one gave me fruit. I remember there was a lady who would fix my hair for me. Good memories.

The next memory I have of being anxious was when I was five. That summer my brother, sister, dad, cousin, his fiancée, and I went to the mountains. We had to pull to the side of the road because my cousin's fiancée had to throw up. Later, after they were married, I was about five when my cousin's wife was talking to my grandma. I must have been pretty smart because I figured out that she was pregnant before they got married because I said something to my cousin- in -law. My grandma told Mom on me. For years up through High school every time they came for a visit I would get stomach cramps and have diarrhea from my anxiety.

My first remembrance of being depressed came when I was in the first grade. I sat in the corner of my bedroom crying after I would come home from school. I attended a Christian school Kindergarten through third grade. It was a very strict environment. We received "Tallies" when we got into trouble. My first grade teacher told me that she could read my mind and that I hated her. It is true that I did not like her, but as I got older, I was able to realize that she could not read my mind, so I was placed in another first grade class where the teacher was much nicer than the first one.

We, also, went to the same church and my Sunday school class teacher said that if you sinned you were not a Christian. I have tried to be perfect my whole life and I still struggle with trying to be perfect. I still feel guilty over things I should not because the Bible says, "For all have sinned and come short of the glory of God." Romans 3:23 KJV.

I went to the eye doctor for the first time while I was in the third grade and got glasses. After the first time I went, I still could not see because I did not tell the eye doctor that things were blurry. Yes, I could see but it was blurry. Then, the second time I went to a different doctor I was able to tell the doctor that my vision was blurry even though I could see. After getting a new pair of glasses, I was amazed at how well I could see.

When I returned to the church, I could see the pastor for the first time. Until that point, I had not seen his face clearly.

I became depressed when I was in the third grade. My mom who was a fifth grade teacher was riding with another teacher to school. The driver asked my mom to get a spider off the front of her dress. When the driver took her eyes off the road just for a second to look down at the spider, she ran off the road into a tree that caused a serious car accident. My dad drove up on the car accident and saw them putting someone in the ambulance and recognized that it was Mom because he could see the new blouse that she was wearing.

When Mom got to the local hospital which was only about two or three minutes away, she insisted that they cut her blouse off in a certain way, so she could wear it again because it was new. Tests showed that her neck had three fractures and almost a severed arm. When mom started to complain of her face becoming numb, the neurosurgeon had her transferred to another hospital that was more suitable to care for her injuries. The surgeon just happened to be a boyhood friend of my dad. They were born in the same mining camp and had been in the same first grade together. Also they had visited in each other's home many times until the doctor's family moved into another town in the state. The doctor, also, told my dad that if the accident had been any harder that my mom would not have survived.

My brother who was eight years older than I and my sister who was six years older than I helped take care of me, so dad could go to the hospital. My next door neighbor also helped take care of me by fixing my hair.

I still remember the day my dad told me about my mom. I was outside in a small swimming pool that was 18 inches deep. I thought my mom was dead since I was too young to go to the Intensive Care Unit. After several days, the nurses in the Intensive Care Unit let me see Mom, and I was greatly relieved to see her alive. However, she had scratches all over her face from the glass in the car. Mom stayed in the hospital for five weeks. Until this day, Dad and I still think about her when we pass by the area where the tree was which is on a daily basis. Someone finally cut down the tree that the car hit, and is not a threat to anyone.

In the fourth grade, I made one of my best friends. When we were little, our parents took turns taking us to each other's houses which was about a twenty five minute drive. Later, when we were in high school, her parents moved into our subdivision about a half a mile from our house that made life easier for all concerned. I managed to go three years without getting depressed or anxious to the best of my knowledge.

While I was in the fourth grade, I switched schools to where my mom taught. In the morning, I would go to the cafeteria with the rest of the students. The group of kids that I hang out with gambled. One day Mom caught a group of students gambling. Although I was not involved, I thought Mom was going to "shoot" me. Another thing that happened was that one morning as we were going into the school, a young man opened the door for us then grabbed mom's purse and ran away. All I was concerned with was that my doughnuts got smashed.

When I was in the fifth grade I developed arthritis in my knees. I remember telling my parents that I wanted to cut off my legs because they hurt so badly. The doctor wanted me to have tests done to see if I had cancer. However, I was greatly relieved when the tests were negative

CHAPTER TWO

Then, came time for me to go to the middle school. While I was in the sixth grade I was in a very disruptive class. Even though the first middle school in which I was enrolled was supposed to be a traditional school with very good discipline, many of the students in class threw paper wads and food. Also, they screamed and yelled a great deal. They even called and ordered pizza delivered to my teacher's house. I told my mom and my dad how bad it was, but they did not believe me. I thought I was having a nervous breakdown. When my mom talked to the principle who was a friend of my parents, he confirmed that what I had said was true, so I was switched to another class and things were not nearly as bad and chaotic. I managed to make passing grades even though they were D's. I think that the teacher gave me passing grades. It was nice being in a quieter class.

I wrote a paper about my experience at Petesdale Middle School in the ninth grade.

Problems at Petesdale Middle School

The day I walked into the building of Petesdale Middle School I really felt good about it. Little did I know that I was going to go through one of the worst experiences of my life. Even now as I look back, it seems like a long nightmare.

As I sat in my chair in Mr. Long's class room, all I could hear were laughter and loud talking. Since I was raised to use self-discipline and had always had teachers who could control a class, this was a new experience for me. I sat astounded not believing my ears as I heard the noise all around me, and not believing my eyes as I saw kids my own age jumping off desks and throwing things. I could not believe the teacher would let this behavior go on. It amazed me how some kids go haywire when they are not disciplined. Luckily, that year I had band. It gave me a chance to have a breather from this awful class.

In class I made all A's, but I knew it was because the teacher was so easy on every one. As I sat in class, the kids around me threw potato chips and gum. It was sickening. I felt awful just sitting there with food in my hair. When I went to the bathroom, I had to comb the yucky stuff out of my hair. Finally, I could take it no more, so I went to the counselor's office to ask if something could be done.

No one believed me. Not even Mom and Dad believed me, so I kept going back to the counselor's office to ask if anything could be done. No one believed me. I kept going back hoping that I would be moved to another class. I gave up on the counselor when she told me, "No," and went to the principle, Mr. Smith. He agreed to at least check in on my problem. He turned the speaker on in the class room and found out that what I said was true. Next, he sent the curriculum coordinator, Mr. Jones, to observe the class. When Mr. Jones came into the class, every one behaved, but as soon as he left, the chaos continued. In my mind,

I did not know if I could take it anymore. Then, the kids began to call me names that I do not want to repeat.

They made fun of my face. They said that I was too good for them and said that I was a tattletale. I thought I was going to have a nervous breakdown from all the pressure from school.

When the semester ended, half of the sixth grade changed classes for all six periods, and the others stayed as they were. I was glad because I figured it would bring some relief from this awful class. After we changed classes, it helped to a degree but it was still wild in Mr. Long's class. After the semester ended, my mom called Mr. Smith to ask him if he would check into this class because she now believed me. It was hard for my parents who, also, were teachers to imagine a teacher or principal letting this go on. They thought I was just having a hard time adjusting to the middle school. Dad, also, talked to a teacher friend who taught in a room where she could observe my class room, and she confirmed what I was saying to be true. Mr. Smith told Mom that it was true about Mr. Long's class control and that is why the students were now changing classes. He, also, told my dad, "Mr. Long is not coming back to this school next year if I have to stand in the door to block him from entering the building." Mr. Smith suggested I be moved to another class. Therefore, I was moved to a different class, and things went much better the rest of the year.

During the summer, I assured myself that the following year would be better. But yet in the back of my mind I still knew that it could happen again. But I wished and prayed that I would not have to go through that again.

Well, the end of the summer came to an end and school started once more. When I walked into my first period class room, the first few weeks went OK, but after that those kids called me names and talked about me behind my back and to my face.

One day in science class this girl, Rita, hit me on the head. It really hurt, and for the first time in all my years of going to school I cried in class. I could not stand it anymore. I know this may sound stupid, but I stood up and called her a name that I should not have called her. I hated her, and I hated the classes.

Rita got on my nerves. That night when I got home, I cried. I told my mom what had happened and she told me the next time someone does that again I have the right to hit that person back as long as I did not hit them first.

Another problem I had was on the bus with a girl named Jennifer. For some reason that I still don't understand, she would call me a very nasty name. When I would be the only one on the bus wearing a blue hat, she would say stuff like "I hate people wearing blue hats." I was fortunate that Jennifer was the only one bothering me. In sixth grade, I always rode the front of the bus, and when I would roll my window down the kids in the back yelled that they hated me. That upset me when I realized that one of the persons went to my church. I can still remember him saying, "I hate you." You may wonder why they made fun of me. Well, it was for several reasons. The first reason was because Petesdale was a preppy school. People said that I was not into the new look that was in. They always made fun of me because I was good. Why would they do that? I really do not know except I was getting A's in conduct and they were getting F's. The last reason is because I was going to the office to tell on the class.

While I attended Petesdale, my academic grades dropped to mostly B's with several C's and one D. At the end of the seventh grade, I begged my mom to let me change schools because I would be in the same classes with these students for a third year because all of the band members were in the same classes all the way through middle school.

When I was in the seventh grade, I accepted Jesus into my heart. I attended a Bible study where I was able to learn more about Jesus. Then, during my eighth grade year, there was a girl in one of my classes that I talked about and made fun of her because the girl's back was crooked. I felt God convicted me to apologize to her for talking about her. However, the conversation did not go very well. Later, when my arthritis got bad, I thought it was God punishing me for doing such a bad thing. In the meantime, I feel like what I went through at Petesdale happens to many kids who do not fit in because they have their own personalities. Different personalities are wonderful because they make a lively world.

Since the new school was my home school, there was not a problem of changing schools. Therefore, the eighth grade and last year in the middle school was a much more pleasant experience. Also, I had arthritis and could ride with my mom to school because she had changed from an elementary school to teach in the local middle school.

My grades improved to A's with the exception of one B. Not only were my grades better, but I, also, had lots of friends.

I had a teacher who told me that I talked too much. He threatened to tell my mom or tell the principle. I begged him to tell the principle because I knew that my mom would "shoot" me if my teacher interrupted her class. Fortunately, for me, he did not tell either one, and things went much better that year.

The End.

CHAPTER THREE

When I was in the eighth grade, I applied to go to a high school that had a traditional program that was stricter and more academically challenging than the regular school, but I was not accepted neither my freshman nor sophomore years because the school had a limited enrolment and there was a long waiting list of students.

In my freshman and sophomore years, I was in the band. The band was in many competitions with other bands in the state. Therefore, I was able to visit several places that I would not have been able to visit. Also, my parents were very supportive of the band and always traveled to see the band compete. On one occasion, from some of the comments that were overheard, my parents felt like that my band did not win any place in the competition because the judges did not like the band director.

In my sophomore year, I fell in love with a guy named John. I liked him. But he did not like me in that way. I got really depressed.

I, also, got depressed when my sister got married and moved to another state. I remember the day my sister and her husband left in their pickup truck. My grades were not affected, but my heart was broken.

It was at this time in my life that I began to get more involved with church. I began reading and praying and keeping a prayer journal. I was very religious. I guess you could call me a Jesus freak.

Today, my daughter and son exhibit that same passion for Christ that I did. They are involved in church and read their Bible daily.

When I was in the third grade, my family joined the church which I attended as a child and a teen ager. At first, Mom was active in the church. She became the Director of the girl's mission study as well as volunteering in the nursery. However, in May of 1979, my mom stopped going to church because she began to have problems with her neck because the bones that were broken in the auto accident had not healed correctly.

As I grew older, I grew more spiritual in Christ. I got involved playing my tuba in the church orchestra, and I joined the bus ministry.

During one of our mission trips, I had several youth sponsors pray over me to get the demons out of me because I hated my mom so much. However, it did not work.

Then, while I was in the ninth grade, I joined the mission's organization for teenage girls. The organization had different levels to earn different steps like a crown, a scepter, a pin, and a cape. In order to earn these steps, a girl must complete service activities. For example, we did back yard Vacation Bible Schools.

During the summer of 1984, I was scheduled to go to a national conference in another state. My mom was supposed to go with me, but she had an accident when she fell through a chair. Her leg became infected, and she had to have surgery, so we asked another Christian woman from church if she would go with me, and she agreed since she had family there, so it worked out well.

That was a great trip. During one of the breaks in the conference, I got to go see my sister's apartment before she did because my brother- in -law had already moved there because of his job.

Also, I learned about a program where high school and college students spent ten weeks doing mission work during the summer.

I applied, and in the summer of 1985 I went on a mission trip and stayed at a mission center with ten other high school and college students from around the country.

The first entry I have started with shows how excited I was to be going.

May 2, 1985

> I am really getting excited now. I have bought the majority of the stuff that I need to buy, so mainly what I need to do now is to pack. I have already made a list for that. If I could, I would leave tomorrow. I can hardly wait until school is out which is not until May 31, 1985.
>
> I am excited. I believe that leaves about 28 or 29 days until I think I can leave. But this summer you, my diary, will probably become my best friend. I like the idea of keeping a diary because years later I can look back and see how things were going now. Then, see the mistakes I made and not repeat them.
>
> Love,
> Nancy

I went back a second summer. Here are some entries from my journal just before my second time as a summer missionary.

May 14, 1986

> This summer will be different than the last summer. I had Bill, my ex-boyfriend. Bill and I dated my sophomore year in high school. He was my first love. I do not remember exactly what happened, but I know it was not good. When

he broke up with me, I had a terrible time. I was sure God wanted us together. After we broke up, I started dating Keith who was four years younger than I. I really liked him. He was a fine Christian teenager and was really mature for his age.

Bill decided he wanted to get back with me, so I broke it off with Keith. Big mistake. I was sure God had placed Bill in my life. I was hurt very badly. As soon as Bill wanted to be together with me, he broke it off again. My heart was broken. Now, I was without Keith and Bill.

Love,
Nancy

May 16 1986

This summer I am free. We will see how this will turn out. Also, I can drive this summer. I plan on riding the bus or van every day and helping with the children. I want to get to know some of the kids better. I want to feel what they feel. I want to be more involved, set better examples, and be in a good mood all of the time. I have changed since last summer for the better. I have been through a lot. I have gotten involved in the bus ministry. This is fun. It all adds up to a growing experience. I praise the Lord for this. We have moved into our new church sanctuary, and I am playing my tuba in the orchestra. These two things have been life changing experiences. I hope that this summer will bring more life changing experiences, and that I will have a growing relationship with the Lord. I, also, hope to meet all of my goals that I have set. I guess I will go for now.

Love,
Nancy

My first summer there we had this horrible van. The door was held shut with a baseball bat. I was scared to death. I was so nervous I sat in the floor of the van when we went out in it. After my mom's accident, she was scared to death riding in a car. I did not want to be that way, but I could not help it. One night the lights in the van went out and we were afraid that someone would pull out in front of us, but we made it back safely. Another scary thing that happened was that one of the guys driving fell asleep at the wheel. I screamed and woke him up. He said that it was God keeping us safe that he woke up because he is normally very hard to wake up.

Also, during that summer, someone broke into the mission center and stole my clothes.

Up until that time, I had been a nail biter. There was another girl there who had beautiful nails. I was determined to let my nails grow out. The first time that I realized I had some nails, I was in Sunday school class. By the next summer, I had let my nails grow out. This was the time before nail salons. I had all colors of nail polish such as blue, purple, red, and green. The kids at the center thought my nails were fake and tried to take them off, but they soon realized that my nails were real.

The second summer we conducted Vacation Bible School, a medical clinic, a clothes closet, and a pharmacy.

One day, I was out of the mission center when my mom called. The other missionaries came and got me to return Mom's call. As we were riding back I began to wonder what had happened. Why was mom in such a hurry to talk with me? Was she calling to tell me that my cat had died? Had my grandpa died? Had something happened to my dad?

Finally, I got back to the center and called her. When we spoke on the phone, she let me know that nothing bad had happened, and that it was good news. The traditional high school had called to tell me that I had finally been accepted to the school, and she needed to call them right away to confirm my acceptance. At this time my mom reminded me that when I signed up to be put on the waiting list that I had prayed if it were God's will for me to go to the traditional school that I would be accepted.

The reason I had signed up my freshman year was because the traditional school had such a fine marching band and I wanted to be part of it. As soon as my mom reminded me of this, I said, "Yes, I'll go." Mom asked me several times if I were positive that I wanted to leave all of my friends, my school activities, teachers who knew me, a field commander position in the band, and the closeness of the school. I said, "Yes," because I knew that God would take care of me as long as I followed His will. It was something I had prayed over the last two years at my regular high school, so I assured her that I would go.

During my second summer at the mission center, we went to a camp at a place called Forever Falls. Forever Falls was a camp for middle school and high school students who went there from all over the state. The camp hosted five thousand campers a week. While I was there, I stopped by a Christian college hut where I learned about a potential college that I might be interested in attending. The school arranged for me to come for a visit. A staff member came to the mission center and picked me up and took me to the college to see the campus where I had the privilege of meeting the president who had been a former pastor here in my home state and was close to my good friend Keith's family and another family in my home church. The university representatives took me to a restaurant for lunch. They, also, offered scholarships to me. I had a really good visit at the university.

I had visited another Christian college in my home state but that college did not offer me the scholarships and the freshman dorm was not air conditioned. Even though my parents had to pay to fly me back and forth on vacations it was still cheaper to go there at 780 miles away from the in-state college.

At that time, we had an exchange student from Germany named John who, also, went to the traditional school and we ended up being good friends. He was like a brother to me. John later married a young lady here in the United Sates, and both became doctors. He became a cardiac anesthesiologist and his wife a pediatrician. They with their three daughters live in the Southeastern part of the United States. Then, in April 2012 my Dad and I flew to the area where they live and spent some time with them. John's mother and his father who is a retired surgeon, also, live near John.

At the same time I was going through my high school blues my Mom was going through a midlife crisis. She told me one day that she was looking for an apartment because "No one appreciates me," as she put it.

On August 2, 1985, I came home from the mission field. Things were crazy at our house. We had an exchange student, my brother, his wife, their son, my parents, my aunt, and uncle were at our house.

I started pre-band camp on August 4, 1985. I was really excited because I knew I was going to meet lots of new people, be in a winning band, and was doing God's will. I really enjoyed pre-band and band camps despite of all the hard work and long days.

When school began, it was a totally different situation. I didn't know very many people and soon discovered that by the time you become a junior or senior you have already become good friends and have your own little group established. I understand this, and I think it is okay, so here I was with very few friends. Neither did I not know who the people were in my classes, nor did I know the teachers. This made school tough not to mention that I had tougher classes such as pre-calculus, chemistry II, and Spanish II. My first six weeks of school were rough. Not only did I have more homework than I was used to doing, but I was, also, having to spend two hours every day after school for band rehearsal and most weekends in band competition.

That year was the first year I became depressed enough to be suicidal. I had it all planned out. My mom still had some valium left in the medicine cabinet, and I planned to take it all. When I told one of my good friends about my feelings, she said to me, "Oh you would never do that," my feelings where hurt. I was trying so hard not to be a burden but the more I thought about it, the more I realized that what I really wanted was to be helped and after I thought about it the more I realized I wanted help and not to die.

The following is a report that was written September 26, 1986, during my senior year. I used the picture of God in a helicopter with myself being in the ocean to describe what I went through during my depression.

During my senior year, I wrote a paper for English entitled "A Time of Fear."

In my life time of seventeen years, nine months, and twenty some odd days, I have never had that ultimate fear that lasted only seconds, minutes, or even hours, but I have had a fear, a different kind of fear that lasted months. One might ask what kind of fear could this be. I'll tell you about this fear. It may be a fear that you have to experience to completely grasp all the feelings involved. Maybe after hearing my story, you might understand it. Perhaps, you might have been there yourself like I was in late June or early July of 1985, when I received the call from my mother about going to the traditional school that was discussed on a previous page when my mom called about my being accepted into the traditional school.

As I already explained, the school was a traditional school where classes were academically harder, and the band was great. It was a school that a student had to apply for entrance. It was a different school than the one that I had been attending. I had prayed about it and felt God was answering my prayer and that that was what God wanted me to do. You see my home school had a small band between 30 and 40 members while the other school had over 100 band members. The new school turned out to be different than I thought. I missed my friends from my home school even though my two best friends went to the traditional school.

While I was there, I met Donald who became my friend. Not because of Donald in any way, but I had a bout of depression and became really depressed. My grades went from A's and B's to D's. I think the teachers gave me passing grades. Donald and I went to prom together, but mine and his were on the same night. Donald wanted to take me to the prom in the student driver's school car. After I said, "No way," Donald borrowed his parent's car. He left the lights on while we were at my prom so, we had to have somebody come and give us a jump.

While attending the traditional school, I became friends with another student who had to go in a psychiatric hospital. I think the reason that he had to go in the hospital was because he had a compulsion to hurt himself by cutting himself.

At the time I had to go to the doctor because I had serious stomach cramps when I woke up in the morning because I was so anxious.

My parents could tell I was not happy because I would cry while watching television. At that time, I was planning on being a missionary and I knew that they did not send any one with mental issues.

Because of the scheduling of the more difficult subjects and two hours of band practice every afternoon, my grades suffered severely. Because of this, I had an F in pre-calculus, a C in Spanish II, and a C in Chemistry II. Now these may not seem like bad grades to some people, but let's consider the fact that I had been an A B student with a 3.6 average at my home school. When my grades fell, the pressure fell from my parents. Now, I cannot and am not blaming my parents for this pressure because it's only their parental duty. In my mind I began to wonder, if I am doing God's will? If I am, then, why am I doing so badly in school? Being the Christian that I am, why am I having such a tough time? Doing God's will is the number one priority in my life. As I began to wonder and ask myself these questions, my thoughts began to get foggy. A great fear or pressure came over me.

During the second six weeks, my grades improved but not by much. By this time, I was getting frustrated with myself. I kept thinking, why don't you do better than this? You know you can. A thought of doubt, am I really doing God's will began to pull me down.

By the end of the third six weeks, I had blown it. I had something like a 55 average for pre-cal. a D in Spanish II and an F in Chemistry II. I, also, had a C in history and English. I felt awful. I kept telling myself that I was stupid, and that I had let my parents down. I had let God down, and letting God down was the worst thing I could ever do. I hated myself. I felt like I was drowning in an ocean in the middle of a foggy night. Finally, what seemed to me the longest semester of my life was coming to an end.

When I got home from school two days before the semester ended, my mother decided that because I was so unhappy at the traditional high school and doing so badly in my classes, that I needed to make the decision of whether I wanted to continue at the traditional school or go back to my home school. She gave me forty-five minutes to decide.

I was so torn that my heart ached. A lot of tears were shed. I was pulled between my best friends at the traditional high school, a terrific band, doing God's will, all my friends at my home school, and good grades. So many fears were running through my mind; a fear of failing my best friends at the traditional school if I left, a fear of failing my best friends at my home school if I stayed at the traditional school, the fear of failing my junior year and having to graduate in 1988, the fear of depression, the fear of going back to my home school and being rejected, the fear of failing my parents, and the greatest fear of all disobeying God.

By this time, I not only felt like I was drowning in an ocean covered with fog, but that I had hold of a rope that was being thrown to me from a helicopter which symbolized God. I kept crying, "God, help me. Please, God help me!" The waves of fear kept splashing hard on me, but I kept on hanging onto the rope with all my might. Finally, I had peace in my heart that I could go back to my home school. On Friday morning, I told my counselor that I was going back to my home school. I was crying the whole time that I was going to her office. After I told her, a big relief came over me.

As I drove to my home school, feelings of anxiety were going through my mind. The closer I got to the school, the faster my heart beat. Walking up the school steps, the fear of returning to my home school entered my mind. After reaching the counselors' office, and having to sit there a few minutes, one of my best friends came to me and gave me a big hug, and my fears were relieved.

Before I went to the traditional school, I had been in classes for college preparation. However, those classes were filled, so I had to go into regular classes. I learned a great deal from the students in those classes. I remember one guy had stinky sneakers which made me almost gag. It is hard to explain but the students in that class seemed to care more about each other than some of the other classes.

That semester I joined the choir instead of the band. I tried out for an extra curriculum choir and I made it not because of my great voice, but because I had great facial expression. We, also, performed at different community events.

During the course of the second semester, my grades came up and improved, but it took me awhile to get back to being my talkative old joking self and regain my self-confidence. By the end of the year, I had been pulled up by God's rope into his helicopter because I kept holding on to my faith in God.

While I was in high school, I met up with a guy named Jack. Jack was younger than I was by about two years. He had one thing that bothered me. He liked to touch me, and I was not that interested in that kind of behavior. One night as we watched a movie on TV, Jack was like Helen Keller in that he liked to touch me with his hands. I did not appreciate his touchiness. Matter of fact, I had even taken a vow to the Lord not to kiss any one until I got married. However, that did not last long. Here are a couple of entries from my journals about Jack:

May 15, 1986

Today was glorious! Praise the Lord! God has blessed me so much! Jack and I had a great time at Kenny's, the youth pastor at the church I attended. We are getting to know each other and it is great. I really like him very much. Today, we discussed about drawing the line when it comes to sex and we both agreed it was super kissing. It is so neat because we have so much in common. We have a dog, like to play sports, but do not like to play Putt Putt. We, also, like to have fun, do not write very much at all, and are both going away this summer.

God has really blessed me. I praise Him so much. Praise the Lord. I guess I better go. It is getting late.

Love,
Nancy

May 17, 1986

Praise the Lord! I had a great day. The time I got to spend with Jack was precious. God has blessed us both so much. When our church had an outing for the younger teenagers, Diane, Todd, Jack and I were asked to be chaperones. We really got a blessing because it ended up that there were more chaperones than were really needed. Therefore, Jack and I did not have to be the chaperones, but got to go along for the fun of it. Then, after we got back Jack came over and we really got to be open to each other. We both like each other very much. We decided we would be devoted to each other this summer. I praise the Lord that Jack is a leader, and a Christian who is growing. This is all I ever asked from God.

Love,
Nancy

During my senior year in high school, my friend Angel introduced me to a guy named Brian. Brian was four years older than I. When we broke up, he became obsessed with me and stalked me. He left notes on my car and front door.

Finally, I had enough. We were in the church parking lot and I went off on him. After that he left me alone.

The following is a note that Brian wrote to me after our break up:

December 8, 1986

Nancy, I am writing this on Sunday. The reason for writing this is not to beg you to come back to me. God answered my prayers yesterday, and I wanted to tell you about it.

When we broke up I was confused. I had never felt so strongly about anyone in my life before. It was hard to understand how two people could end up with such different feelings. For two weeks, I have had many sleepless nights. I was everything on the road. I drove by your house and church countless times just hoping to see you.

I have had thoughts of sending you flowers or leaving them on your car at church with a sad note. Thank the Lord He showed me how thoughtless that would be. After many prayers of begging God to bring you back to me, it hit me that I was praying only for myself and not for you. Before I go on, let me back up and tell you that if it had not been for God showing me how much he loves me and how much I needed to work for Him and for people to see Him in me I would not have made it. This Friday night I decided I had to pray for both of us. I told God how much I care for you and that I now could understand that it must have been hard for you to tell me your feelings and I now know that you did not want to hurt me. That's when I asked God to tell me weather I needed to try and get you back with everything I had or to let you go or make it harder on you. Saturday, He gave me this feeling that I had to let you go. The last thing I want to do is to hurt you. God is right. I saw a poster that said "If you love something, set it free. If it comes back to you, it's yours if not it never was." I think it could be true here. I really do not know how to say this but it is on my heart and I would not rest until I do. I have let it go today. God never really told me but I still think it is OK the way I feel about you. I'll try to go out and date, but I want you, also, even though it hurts so much. I think I can say "I love you." and maybe by dating I will change my mind. I really hope I do not have to I, also, wanted to tell you, setting what I just said aside, that whatever happens to us knowing I have got such a great Christian sister is something that God will always bless me with. I want you to know that you can call me anytime as a Christian friend because no matter how many churches we are all one big family. I hope that someday we can get back together. Please call me whenever you just need to talk or would like to try it again. I hope I have not hurt you with this letter but all of this was heavy on my heart.

I love you in Jesus,
Brian

Chapter Four

I started hallucinating in my junior year of high school. I thought my mom was Satan. I mean I really thought Mom was Satan sent by God to test me. I hated my mom.

Here is an entry from my journal about my feelings about my mom.

May 18, 1986

> Mothers! I cannot stand them! They get on my nerves. My mother thinks she can tell me what to do. Well of course she can. But I do not have to like her. But God is not done with me yet. I pray that God will help me to love her.
>
> Love,
> Nancy

My best friend and a youth minister told me I was not a Christian because Christians love everybody and do not hate anyone. I would look in the mirror and see a skull in place of my face. That was really scary.

In 1985, I began to think that I was hearing things which is called auditory hallucinations. I was walking down the street behind my house when I heard a voice saying, "Tell that lady about Christ or she will go to hell." I never told that lady. Then, while I was babysitting three handicapped children who lived in a three story house, I began hearing noises from upstairs like the closet door opening and shutting. I knew it was not the children because they were all in wheel chairs. I never told anyone about these strange things that happened to me. I just chalked it up to God.

Another hallucination was about a pot hole in the road. Every time I hit it I would think that I killed someone and I would listen on the radio to see if there had been a hit and run. Years later, the road department finally repaired that pot hole. I, also, believed that if I listened to secular music in my car, I would wreck. Therefore, I only listened to Christian music.

As I grew older, my depressions increased in length and in intensity. One time I was driving my friends to an event in down town the day after Thanksgiving. When I hit something in the road, I pulled over and made one of the guys get out and look to see if I had done any damage to the car. Fortunately, I did not do any damage. Another misfortune I had driving was when I was driving in a school parking lot and I hit a curb and my car became air born. These are two things I never told my parents, but I guess my dad knows now.

My senior year in high school I got involved back in band. I fell in love with my band director. At the end of the year, I wrote him a letter explaining my feelings about him. When I gave him the letter I gave him the wrong one. He started reading it and I realized it was the wrong letter, and I was really embarrassed.

I always have had feelings about starving since I was about five or six when I refused to eat. That year I became obsessed with my weight. I only ate Snickers bars and diet drinks from the coke machine. I lost down to 117 pounds and I was five feet and five inches tall. I was probably on the borderline of anorexia. I remember feeling great when I did not eat. It was like I felt great to feel starved. However, after eating more, I finally got up to 130 pounds.

CHAPTER FIVE

Well, the day came to move in to college. When I arrived, I saw someone who had brought a UHAUL trailer. I could not believe that someone would bring a UHAUL to the dorm. Wouldn't you know it was my roommate.

College was totally different than home. I was free to do what I wanted. Dating boys in college was much different than dating in high school. One day I had two dates in a day. One night I had a scheduled date with a guy I was half way interested in. I told the first guy whom I went out with that my roommate had to get up early the next day, and I had to get back early, so that I would not wake her up because she needed to get up early. But the second guy that night won my heart over. His name was Mike who was a year ahead of me. We started dating and pretty soon we were in love. We dated all of my freshman year and my sophomore year.

During the summer between my freshman and sophomore years, Mike cheated on me with a girl he knew from high school in his home town. He cried on the phone and he felt really remorseful which was enough for me. Then, he flew with me to meet my family during our Spring Break in 1989 of my sophomore year. One night at the dinner table Mike asked my dad if he could marry me. Then, when my dad said, "Yes," he turned to me and asked me to marry him. I said, "Yes," at the time, but I knew in my heart that I was not going to marry him.

Mike was a smooth talker, but when it came to knowing him he was a very jealous person. I can remember one day when we were walking across campus when a workman came and asked me if I knew of any one who had lost a key. Because I was a Resident Assistant in the dorm, he thought I might know of someone. After the man passed, Mike told me that he did not want me to talk to any one like that again.

During the Spring Break that Mike came home with me, I went to my rheumatologist because my arthritis that I had had since I was a kid was causing me problems, and I had mono. The doctor gave me some medications to treat both my arthritis and my mono.

I had stopped answering Mike's phone calls. My mom had always told me never to go in a guy's room and Mike's parents asked us to go into his room when we were at his parents' house. One night two weeks before the end of the Spring semester in 1989 I told Mike I did not know if I wanted to marry him or not. Mike then, told me that the courtship was over, and he did not want to be together any more. We spoke three times after that. Mike had bought a truck because I liked trucks, so he was reminded of me when he drove it, and I felt good about that.

I called my parents at midnight to tell them about my break up. My mom said that it was the medicine that caused me to feel that way. The hardest part getting disengaged was when I had to return my engagement ring to Mike. It made my disengagement feel so final. I still loved him and mourned over him.

That summer I worked at a hardware store, and I craved men's attention. I wore short skirts and flaunted myself. There was one guy whom I fell in love with at the hardware store.

But he just wanted to be friends. Again, I lost weight from 130 pounds to 117 pounds and went to a size five.

Because I had planned on going to the mission field, I was on a scholarship at the university. Because of that, it was required that I be involved in a church and have a document signed by the pastor of the church. The church I was involved in had about 25 members. When it came time for the pastor to sign the form, he denied that I had ever been involved in the church even though I had sung solos, worked with the youth group, and had helped out with the nursery. My feelings were hurt because this was the man who was supposed to have performed our wedding ceremony. I told the university about my situation and they told me to have my home church to fill out the form, so I did. Even though I never went into the mission field, I have never been questioned about my service. However, I am now on Social Security Disability Income and cannot work at the time of this writing.

When I went back to school in the fall of 1989, I was severely depressed. I remember the night I thought I was having a nervous breakdown. I shared an on campus apartment with three other girls. I was in my room with the door shut screaming out to God and crying. My roommates called the supervisor and she came out pretty fast. She came into my room and asked me if I knew where I was and what was going on. I told her, "Yes," on both questions. The next day, the head of women's housing called me in and told me if I did not get help she was going to call my parents. I told her I had already made an appointment with a preacher whom I will call BJ.

We met ten times. One of the hardest things I had to do was to name ten good things about myself because I had very low self-esteem and I still do today.

I, also, had issues with my mom. I felt like she was trying to control me. Another issue was when I was out in public I would see myself out side of my body. BJ told me to go home and sleep it off. That was a scary time in my life. BJ told me he probably should have sent me to a psychiatrist, but he thought he could help me. However, he did tell me that he was in over his head.

To this day, I still have dreams that contain my going to the university to work on my master's degree, so I could be close to my children. In my dream, I am a Resident Assistant who forgets to do her job. In the end, I always lose the job. Dad told me recently that if he had known how depressed I was that he would have come to the university and brought me home. At the present time, Betty attends the same university that I did.

While I was a Resident Assistant in the apartments on campus, I roomed with a girl whom I'll call Joy who was deeply depressed. The apartments slept four. Each apartment had two bed rooms and two bath rooms. Every time I went into the apartment I checked the bath room to make sure she had not hanged herself. I, also, lived with the same girl for two and a half years, the same girl who had brought the UHAUL. Although, I did not like her, we tolerated each other. Our senior year she moved off campus. That year I had three new roommates. I had my own room when one of the girls left after she completed the fall courses she needed.

During my junior year, I was so depressed that I came back home during my Fall Break and toured a school and had to decide if I were going to return to my current school or change to the local school, but I decided to continue at my current school.

CHAPTER SIX

During my senior year, I started dating Nick. Nick and I do not remember meeting, but we remember that the youth group from the church where we attended had a lot to do with getting us together. Our first date was in November 1990. Later in our date, we went to Nick's parents' house. The first time I met Nick's extended family and friends was at his dad's fiftieth birthday party in January 1991. This was an event that I'll never forget. After that we spent a lot of time talking on the phone. We, also, sat in his car listening to a CD player which he had purchased, and had hooked up to his cassette player in his car.

One night, Nick and I talked about getting married, but made a mutual decision not to tell anyone. I remember the first time Nick told me he loved me. We were in his apartment dancing. When he told me he loved me, I told him that it scared me because I thought I loved him too. The reason it scared me was because I had loved Mike, but things had not turned out as I had planned. I was really hurt when Mike and I broke up. In March, Nick and I talked about getting married. Nick was very handsome. He had great legs and a great body. I, also, had great legs that were slender and tan.

Nick asked me to marry him one Wednesday after church during spring finals in 1991, and he gave me a wonderful tear drop sapphire ring with diamonds around one side of it. I love sapphires, and I had dropped him hints that was what I wanted. I loved that ring. He even had the proposal taped. I purchased a wedding band with a diamond in it to match the engagement ring, but I had the diamond removed. The two rings matched perfectly, and I decided to have them attached to one another. When I went to pick up the rings, I was in for a shock because the jeweler had attached them backwards. I went to the store in the mall where Nick's sister worked and cried because it was backwards. Fortunately, they were able to correct it before my wedding. After the divorce, I sold the rings to my sister.

Nick and I had devoted our lives to the ministry; Nick to youth ministry and myself to social work for a Christian based organization in the United States. However, after we started dating we both decided to pursue other occupations. Nick changed his major to art, so he could do graphic arts, and I changed my major to family counseling with a minor in anthropology. My mom blamed Nick for my changing careers and his parents blamed me for Nick changing careers, but the truth is we changed them together.

Nick had one problem. He was a controller, and reminded me of my mom. During Spring Break of my senior year in 1991, Nick came to meet my family. While he was there, he and my sister got into a water fight in the kitchen with the water sprayer from the sink and things just did not go well from then to the end of the visit. After the water fight, Nick did not talk to anyone but me.

Nick was a really good cook. He even made chocolate pretzels for me. I remember the first year we dated Nick lived in an apartment on campus at the university. He had three roommates.

Nick decorated his apartment with Christmas lights on the ceiling.

Nick was not a smooth talker like Mike had been. Mom tried to tell me that Nick was revengeful. Nick's parents did not like me and my family did not like the way that Nick treated me. During that time, I realized that Nick was full of revenge. Later, during our divorce that trait was nearly unbearable. However, my love for him was so strong that I did not ask God if we should get married because my break up with Mike was so painful that I did not think I could take another break up. Nick was a year behind me in school and his parents were paying for his tuition. Therefore, we set our wedding date for the summer, of 1992.

CHAPTER SEVEN

When I graduated from college in 1991, I did not have a job, and life was hard financially. Also, the two girls I was living with were hard to deal with. Then, one more girl moved into our house, and actually slept with her boyfriend which I did not approve of this situation.

In the meantime, my parents drove to my place. While they were there, they cleaned the house really good and painted the house. We had fleas which I am allergic to in our house. They were so bad that I could literally see them on my white comforter. One of my roommates had a cat that went outdoors, since the house next door had no one living in there with high grass in the lawn this made the fleas worse.

While living in that house, I purchased a lawn mower that had to be put together. Nick and I realized that we could not do projects together. I tried to put it together and ended up with the handle upside down. Nick tried to tell me that it was upside down but I did not believe him until I tried to run the mower.

Finally, it came down to one of my roommates deciding to move back into the dorm. Because I could not live on my own financially, I had to find a place that I could afford. When we lived in that house it did not have a refrigerator, Therefore, I rented a small one for $40.00 a week. I ended up purchasing one on credit from a local appliance store where my payments were $28.00 a month. The refrigerator came back to haunt me because we never used that refrigerator again, and it always ended up in storage. It took me what seems like forever to pay it off. Right after I moved and did not need it anymore, some friends of ours took the refrigerator, and stored it for us. They, also, had our table and chairs.

In the process of looking for the refrigerator, I went into a furniture store. While I was in the store, the sales manager asked me if I would like a job. Since I did not have one I said, "Yes." However, I am not a born sales person. Therefore, working there was hard. Then, one day, the sales manager asked me if I would be in a commercial for the store, but I had to decline because I got a new job as the custodian at the church I was attending. My mom told me she was embarrassed of her daughter who had a college degree working as a custodian. But the way I looked at the situation it was paying the bills. I enjoyed the job because I could wear shorts and listen to music. I was really good at cleaning. I used a tooth brush to clean around the faucets. One of the members would put trash behind doors to see if I were cleaning there.

Because I did not have an automobile at that time, Nick's parents gave me a car after they bought a new one. I thought that was really nice of them. Before that, I had to walk almost everywhere I went. The laundromat was about a mile away, so I was grateful for the car.

When I went to look for an apartment, all I could find were nasty apartments. Finally, I was about to give up when I read in the want ads an advertisement that read "clean apartment". When I went to look at the apartment, it was old but it was nice and clean, so I moved in it. My rent was $175.00 a month. I did not have a phone because one of my roommates ran up a $400.00

phone bill that was in my name, and I could not afford to pay it off. Finally, my mom and my dad paid the bill for me.

Also, I was afraid of the men out side of my apartment building because they were bums, homeless men living at the homeless shelter across the street. Nick and a roommate moved into an apartment building next door which made me feel safer.

Back to my job at the church. One time the minister, BJ, asked Nick to look outside and down my shirt. Also, at various times he tickled me which was very inappropriate for a minister. Nick finally told him that he needed to stop looking at me and use his brain. Since we had asked him to perform our wedding ceremony, Nick and I decided to have BJ and the music minister at the church where Nick grew up to share the ceremony.

In August 1991, I got a call from a mental health agency wanting to hire me for a position where I helped adults with mental illnesses such as schizophrenia and depression, to get jobs, train them on the job, and helped them keep their job. There was one particular guy that got a job at a local chain store stocking third shift. He was having difficulty getting his job done on time, so I drew him a map of the area where he worked and gave him a list of what to do. Because he followed these ideas, he was able to keep his job. I was even filmed and was put into a promotional video about my job.

I moved in with a friend of Nick's who was living in her grandma's house, and shared living expenses. One day she came home with a poodle.

I figured if she could have a dog I could too. However, my roommate's mom did not think the same way, but she let me keep the beagle.

I loved my job, and I loved Nick. I had the best year of my life during that first year after I graduated from college. I did well at work, and I got to talk to Nick on the phone many times. Also, we visited back and forth because the university was only about thirty minutes away from where I lived with Debbie.

Mom came down during that year to help me pick out a wedding dress. The one I liked was about three thousand dollars which was too expensive for me. A friend of mine ended up making my wedding dress. I took some pictures out of a magazine that had pictures of wedding gowns, and she made the dress from my pictures that I picked out. She hand sewed over four hundred beads on my dress and only charged me $400.00. This was a lot less than the dresses I had chosen. It was off the shoulder with puffy sleeves. It was straight with a split up the back with lace and beads.

Nick and I were married in the summer of 1992. The music was excellent and there were only two glitches. First, I lost the wedding license which after we looked for it all over that house I called the license office to say we had lost the license. They told me I would have to get a notarized letter stating that we had lost it. So I called the church to see if the notary public could do it but unfortunately the electricity was out. My mom later told me she had it in her purse. The electricity was on by the time we had our dress rehearsal.

Then, came the second blooper. Annie made my train fifteen feet long and made it with Velcro, so I could take it off during the reception after my twin nephews who were about five years old carried the train down the aisle to the altar. However, I really did not want a train. After my dad gave me away, he accidentally stepped on my train as I took a step forward at the same time he turned to go to his seat. The audience heard a ripping sound and saw the train fall to the floor. During the prayer, Nick's father who was seated next to the aisle reached down and pulled it to him as if it had been planned. This sent my brides' maids laughing. I told Nick that I thought my train had come off, and sure enough it had. I was just glad it had come off, so I did not have to worry about tripping over it when I went up the steps to the stage. My dad felt horrible, but to me that was the best thing that could have happened. What was even funnier was that people thought that I had planned it that way. One of my other two nephews carried the Bible and the other my ring pillow which Annie finished the cross stitch ring bearer pillow.

Before the ceremony, the wedding party sat in the reception hall just taking it easy. I had a cake shaped like a computer made for Nick because he was really into computers. I had a cake that was really pretty and tea to drink because I do not like punch.

After we stayed at the reception, we went to leave and found that Nick's friends used shaving cream to paint on our car "just married". Nick got really mad and showed the ugly side of himself. I do not know why he got so upset because our car was a 1978 Chevy. By the time we got to the hotel Nick had calmed down.

When we got to the hotel, one of the groomsman had a bottle of Champaign waiting for us. Nick and I tasted it, but decided that we did not like it, so we emptied the bottle down the drain. On the night of our honeymoon, we went back to our house that we were renting to see my parents before they left town the next day because my mom had insisted that we come to see them before they went back home. We only stayed one night at the hotel because we were broke, but Nick had joined some travel club which gave us a free night at the hotel. When we left the hotel, I accidentally left some lingerie that I never got back.

Chapter Eight

Nick and I had a large credit card debt when we married. Between the two of us we had ten credit cards. When I got pregnant, I was uninsured because I chose not to utilize cobra which made me have to pay $10,000.00 because my pregnancy was preexistent to my new insurance. The finance lady at the OBGYN told me we had to pay $100.00 a month until we got it paid. I told her "You cannot squeeze blood out of turnip." Her response was, "No. but we can sue your turnip." We ended up with over $30,000.00 in debt, so we chose to go to credit counseling. For the small fee of $15.00 a month they lowered our payments. The credit counseling made the checks and sent them for us when we gave them a money order. When Nick and I divorced, the judge ordered Nick to take over the payments, and he finally got the debt paid off after seven years.

In the beginning of our marriage, I used birth control pills. In August 1992, I began to get depressed. I thought it was my birth control pills. So I went back to the doctor, but he refused to change my pill, so I went off of them. I felt really guilty because I had never told Nick about my depressions because I had never thought about it being a problem even though I had gotten depressed and anxious many times.

CHAPTER NINE

Nick decided that we should move to my home town to live. He had this big idea that the computer graphics jobs were better in my home town than his home town. He had plans to make my dad's shed into a work shop. However, things did not turn out to be the way he planned.

When we started thinking about moving, I had the newspaper from my home town sent to my house where I was living. I found a job that I was interested in. I got a job by phone interview at the local homeless shelter as an employment counselor with homeless families who moved out into the community. However, it was hard to look for a job for clients who would frequently change their mind.

When Nick and I first moved to my home town, we moved in with my parents. Our room was in the basement. Nick and I referred to it as the dungeon. After living there about six weeks, we found a nice house to rent. However, the house was not big enough. I got pregnant in November because we were not careful with our method of birth control. When I went into the kitchen, I had to literally lift my belly up over the kitchen table.

We had one of the worst landladies that a renter could have. We had two beagles when we moved into the house. We did not think of it as a problem because the ad in the paper did not say anything about pets, so we figured it was OK. When the property owner found out about our pets, she was quite upset. Another thing she was upset about was leaves in the back yard. She made me rake the leaves in January 1993.

During our six years of marriage, we moved thirteen times. Six of those moves were in our first year of marriage.

When Nick and I decided to move to my home town, we did not have the money, so we borrowed it from my parents. Later, when I received my back pay from Social Security Disability, Nick would not let me repay my parents, so my mom paid my brother and sister the same amount as we had borrowed from them.

We had purchased a couch from a local store for $600.00 to match an old love seat, and it turned out to be a terrible sofa. When my friend told me my couch looked pretty good to be used, we knew we needed to take it back, and we did. When we got moved, we went to a cheap furniture store and purchased two rocking chairs and a couch. However, when we moved into our rental house our furniture was bigger than the space we had.

My depression got really bad. One night, while we were moving into our house I cried so hard that I had to have someone come pick me up. After that I went through the phone book looking for a counseling service that was prorated. I found a person who said that he specialized in depression. He even told me that he had written a book and led a group for depression. But he had one problem; he fell asleep during our sessions. After I went to him for ten weeks, he finally told me that I needed to go get my hormones checked, so I did. The doctor told me to come back the next week for the results of my blood work. In between the week I went to the doctor and my return visit Nick told me he thought I was pregnant. So I took two pregnancy tests and they both showed I was pregnant. When I went back I told the doctor and sure enough I was pregnant. This was two weeks before Christmas. When I went back to the counselor whom I had told every session that I hated my job, he told me that I had never told him about hating my job. This counselor, also, told me that whenever I mentioned suicide to him he thought about taking me to a local hospital. Therefore, I never went back because I wasn't suicidal. I was just consumed by the idea of dying.

Nick and I were financially poor. In February 1993, I got a new job at a local mental health center working with adults who have mental illnesses such as schizophrenia and depression at a club house where the members at the clubhouse worked to keep it going. I really liked my job. It was a good match, and I got to work with mentally ill adults which I felt was my calling.

My first day there was very memorable because for lunch we had pizza which made me sick. While I was pregnant, every time Nick ordered pizza I made him go into another room because the smell of pizza made me sick. I remained depressed my whole pregnancy. I would lie in bed or on the couch crying myself to sleep. Nick said I kept him awake when I was crying in bed because we had a water bed and I made the bed shake. Nick was not the comforting type.

Because Nick and I realized that we could not live on our own with the cost of having a baby, we asked my parents if we could move in with them and pay them rent, so in July 1993, we moved in with my mom and my dad.

Chapter Ten

Our daughter, Betty, was born on August 25, 1993 and weighed a whopping 10 pounds and 2 ounces. She was a great baby. She began to sleep through the night beginning at two weeks. I had a private babysitter who only charged $40.00 per week, which was a bargain compared to $80.00 a week that day care centers cost. She, also, let us save money by letting us use cloth diapers. One week that we did not have the money to pay our baby sitter I thought that God made it snow 18 inches, so that I could stay home to keep Betty and not have to pay the baby sitter. Later, I found out that God would not make it snow just for one person. I started back to work after four weeks after Betty was born in late summer of 1993, and my depression worsened.

In the fall of 1993, I had all I could stand living with my parents. It was stressful and our finances were even more strained because Nick had gotten a job that was supposed to give him 40 hours a week, but it ended up being more like 20 hours a week.

I called my employee counseling services and got an appointment in two days. I think the man I talked to about getting an appointment could tell I was overly stressed. When I went for my appointment, I met my therapist who helped me to figure out that I have Schizoaffective Disorder because I have a running commentary which is like having a radio announcer in my head that

I can't shut off. I enjoyed working with Margaret because she was definitely different than other counselors. Schizoaffective Disorder is a psychotic disorder with a mood disorder such as depression in my case. I once had a psychiatrist that asked me if I ever wished that I was bi-polar because at least I would feel high some time.

I was able to get a job working from 6:00 until 8:00 a.m. in a daycare to make ends meet.

I got a discount for Betty and was able to spend some quality time with her in the mornings. We still had our 1978 car, and Nick for whatever reason put an alarm on it. However, the alarm was messed up, and as I was driving down the road, the alarm was going off at 5:45 in the morning. After I was in the day care, someone came into the day care and told me my alarm was going off, but there was nothing that I could do. Believe me that was quite embarrassing to me.

Soon, I realized that with my extra job that we could move out on our own. We began looking at apartments. We found one that only cost $275.00 a month. After living there a while, we realized why it was so cheap. It was next to a sewer plant which on occasion backed up into our bathtub. The gross thing about it was that pink toilet paper came into our bathtub when we only used white. One time, Nick's parents came to our apartment for a visit, and our apartment flooded while they were visiting us.

I had a sinus infection for about ten weeks. When the carpet people came to replace the old carpet, there was a great deal of mold under the carpet. No wonder I stayed so sick for so long. Once we moved out into another apartment I got well.

In the summer of 1994, my best friend killed herself by carbon monoxide poisoning. I cried for days while I was at work. I would go to the bathroom and sit on the floor and cry. We had been together the week before. We were riding in her car when she got a flat tire on our way to go fishing with the men in our lives. She had a boyfriend, and I had a husband. We sat on the banks of a river while our men fished.

Kathy and I talked about how we wanted to die. We felt cheated because of our illnesses having a negative effect on our lives. She, also, suffered from Depression, and I endured Anxiety, Depression, and Schizoaffective Disorder. I do not know if the flat tire caused her to do what she did or not. I was devastated. Kathy was the only one in my life who truly knew how I felt. I grieved greatly over her loss because she was one of my very best and closest friends. I still to this day think about her when I either see a car like hers or somebody who looks like her.

I went to my family doctor for medicine for my Depression for about six months. One day, I told him that I thought my husband was leaving the windows unlocked so that someone could come in and kill me. Then, he told me that I needed to see a psychiatrist. Therefore, I agreed to go to a psychiatrist at the mental health clinic.

The following entry is from the first psychiatrist that to whom I drudgingly went.

February 7, 1995

I went to the doctor tonight. He increased my medicine, and we had a chat. He said that there are four areas in a person's life which are spiritual, financial, physical, and emotional. I told him that I had given up on God, so I did not know if I could meet that aspect of the four areas. I can tell I am thinking a little better because my thoughts have slowed down.

Love,
Nancy

The medication that I was on made my knee shake. While Nick's parents were here, I told them that I was on medication for depression which caused my knee to shake. Nick's dad proceeded to tell me that it was my fault that I got depressed. He told me that I chose to get married when I did, and I chose to have Betty when I did. I was six months pregnant on our one year anniversary.

I felt so misunderstood by everyone. They did not know how much pain I was enduring. I went to take a shower and I screamed and cried while I was in the shower. I did not realize that Nick's parents could hear me until Nick got home from work and he talked to his parents about me. I was embarrassed, misunderstood, and ashamed. Nick's dad never has understood my illness. I believe that he is afraid of me because when I went to stay with Nick's parents' for the week end, which I will explain in the book later, he would lock the door to his bedroom.

The following excerpt comes at a time when I was feeling sorry for myself.

February 10, 1995

I just cannot figure out what I have done to deserve this. The Bible says in Galatians 6:7 KJV. "Be not deceived; for whatsoever a man soweth, so shall he reap." I am just feeling sorry for myself and I would regret it. Maybe, I should list good things then, I would feel better with Nick's parents about my depression I could have talked to his parents more in depth about my illness. But I feel like it would fall on deaf ears

Love,
Nancy

CHAPTER ELEVEN

In July 1994, I enrolled in a master's program through one of the Northeast's universities where I could earn credit while working on my job. Matter of fact, one of the requirements was that one had to be able to work and use your current clients to do the program. I had to fly to the university, so my mom let me mow the grass and in return she paid for my plane ticket. I had to go two weeks in the summer and two weeks in January 1995.

Things went pretty good in the summer. In the meantime, I was promoted at work. Therefore, I got to quit my day care job which made life easier for me. When the supervisor at work quit, I was put me in charge as co-director. When another coworker quit, I had to work by myself and the stress level sky rocketed. However, it gave me a $6000.00 a year raise. Because I received a thousand dollar stipend from school, I hired someone to clean our apartment. That was the most well spent money I have ever had. Here is a journal entry from that time.

February12, 1995

Today was a pretty relaxed day. I got my homework done and mailed. Getting my house cleaned by Loretta was the best thing I have done for myself. At least one area in my life is under control and less overwhelmed. Nick kept our apartment very cluttered. We had papers and bills everywhere. We had dishes stacked all over the kitchen. Our bedroom looked like clothes were thrown all over our room. Loretta was a great cleaner. However, she could not wash our clothes, so she just piled all of our dirty clothes in a corner of our bed room.

Love,
Nancy

At one time, Nick and his mom claimed that I had bills in the couch, and scattered around the house. I am sure I am not the only one who did that.

In January 1995, I went back to the university for another two weeks. The teachers were not happy with the class and got on to us. At this time I was not feeling very well at all. I was worried that people could tell that I was having problems. Here is a journal entry from that first week:

January 11, 1995

I sat and was miserable because I felt so bad. I was self-conscious of shaking which has calmed down now. I guess I feel at times that people can read my mind, and they know either I am depressed or that I get depressed. I am so afraid of God, and I reason through what He might interpret my prayers to hurt me that I finally just stopped praying. I know that I told my therapist that I thought maybe the medicine would help me which it has, but I still cannot pray. You know what I miss most about God? It is the hope that I used to have that He could make everything better. Now I know He cannot, and I just cannot figure out what I did for Him to allow me to suffer. I know it could be worse, but there is nothing worse than losing my mind. See, I feel like I just jinxed myself and that Nick and Betty will be hurt. See I live in fear of God. You know maybe there are demons in me. What is a crazy person supposed to do? Oh, I know that I am not crazy. But I feel out of control of my head.

Love,
Nancy

January 18, 1995

Well, here I sit at a restaurant. I worked very hard this week reading all the articles from Cathy's class. I wanted to say something, so I decided to write in my journal to help me express myself.

I talked to Mark, one of the professors, I received an A in his class. I was very proud of myself. We talked about my depression, and he told me he was glad I talked to him about it in case my illness began to interfere with my work as a student.

Now, I am trying to study for Matthew's class. I am reading the material, so I can be prepared. I am having a hard time focusing. I am worried about going crazy. I just have to keep telling myself everything is going to be OK and these are just feelings and bad thoughts running through my head. I think I might be getting paranoid thoughts again because I feel people know that I am on ten zillion medicines when reality says that they cannot read my mind.

I feel I am kind of immature. I keep getting these feelings and sensations like I am floating the whole time from eight o'clock and it is now eleven o'clock. I am sure it is distress and stress combined with exhaustion put together with being away from home. If I did not have to study, I would go to sleep.

I just have to keep reassuring myself these are feelings and not my state of mind, or else I would not be able to tell the difference. I am OK, and I will be alright.

Love,

Nancy

In the summer of 1995 I had to give up my school program because I was not working. I never went back. I was the only student that they had that had quit the program. I borrowed $20,000.00 for my schooling. When I became disabled with my mental illness, my loan was forgiven in 1996.

CHAPTER TWELVE

I helped Nick to get a job at the agency for which I was working. But he just did not understand the responsibilities of the job. He was a Job Coach which helped people with mental illnesses to obtain a job and keep it.

My sister's family member endured bi-polar condition. When my sister told us about her experience, Nick laughed. Then, my sister told him if it were his family member he would not think it was funny.

January 22, 1995

Nick told me that he thought the reason that God had given him a new job working with people with mental illnesses was so he could understand my depression more than he already understood it. I started to say you could have asked me, but I did not say anything. The idea that he is interested in me means a lot more. I love Nick.

Love,
Nancy

Nick had three different jobs within the company for which I worked. They all complained about him to me. In 2004, when I went to work at one of the places he had been, the staff was not complimentary of his work ethic.

My therapist at that time called Nick in to tell me how he would feel if I would kill myself, but Nick just sat there. He did not say anything. She even prompted him, and he said nothing.

This did not help my paranoia. I had already thought that Nick was leaving the windows unlocked for someone to come in and kill me.

At that time I was experiencing many symptoms. When I would drive, I would feel like I was going to pass out. I had a time when I was driving with a client and I had to pull over because I thought I was going to pass out. I had a running commentary which talked to me nonstop. That running commentary is what helped us decide that I had Schizoaffective Disorder. The best way to describe it is like having a radio announcer in my head making comments about everything I did. For instance it might say, "There she goes walking across the room, watch how she moves. She is cleaning. There is a spot that she missed, and some body is trying to trick her."

I was suicidal. I thought that I was dead and all that was left of me was my spirit. When I was sitting down, I saw my body outside of me. That really scared me. I felt like I had a knife sticking out of my back. I believed that people could read my mind. I again became suicidal. The psychiatrist put me on an anti-psychotic medicine in January 1995 which knocked me for a "loop". I just laid there on the couch for three days. However, it did help with the running commentary. The next insert is from January 18, 1995. I discuss the hard ship of working by myself.

January 18, 1995

Well, today was better than yesterday. Perhaps it was because my new supervisor called and hired someone to come and help me after we lost $700.00 because I was not billable, and my other coworker was on vacation. Cathy, also thanked me for doing a good job and keeping up the billing. It was hard for me to accept the credit for something, but it did feel good that she recognized my efforts of still working. Of course, she doesn't know of my struggles to keep on working. I don't want to tell her because I am afraid she may think bad thoughts of me. When I think about it, I guess it is hard for me to admit that I really do have less respect for people who have depression or other mental illnesses. Maybe "respect" isn't the word I am looking for, but maybe, that it is that I don't trust them or rather I can't depend on them as much because of their illnesses, so that is how I expect people to see me. I am worried that is what people will view me as a burden, someone that they have to tip toe around. I know that it is hard for other people like Nick who doesn't get depressed to understand what I go through. I get saddened looking forward to a future when I don't get depressed about getting depressed. One of the things that my friend who killed herself and I used to sit around talking about was how that it is frustrating that when we should be doing our best we cannot because we become depressed.

Love,
Nancy

I sat in school and was miserable because I felt so badly. I was self-conscience of my legs shaking which has calmed down now. I guess I feel at times that people can read my mind, and they know my prayer to not hurt myself and my family that I finally gave up praying. I told Melissa that maybe praying would help me which it has, but I still can't pray. Do you know what I miss about God? I can't figure out what I did to cause Him to allow me to suffer like I do. I know that the hurt could be worse. See, I live in fear.

Then, I started missing work because I could not get out of bed. I got to the point where I would not even call into work until the afternoon. I talked to my supervisor who was very supportive. She told me that I should go to the hospital if that is what my doctor wanted. She just wanted me to get well.

January 24, 1995

Today, I took the day off because I was just too tired to go to work. I actually got up and took a shower. Yesterday, I didn't do anything at work except stress management class and a few notes. I couldn't sleep very much and I haven't been too hungry. When I did sleep, I had bad dreams. Betty stayed home with me today because Nick had physical therapy.

I put Betty in her bed and let her play. Nick was nice to me today and said that he wasn't mad at me for staying home. I think he is actually an honest man. If I could just believe him that would actually relieve my mind of him leaving me some day. I sat on the couch today and read Betty *Elmo Takes a Bath* or "Melmo" as she calls him. I didn't have the energy to play with her, but I could sit on the couch with her. That seemed as though I am not able to enjoy her right now which makes me sad.

I am trying to actually pray again. All I can say is God forgive me of my sins. Help me to feel better and don't let me die.

Love,
Nancy

February 2, 1995 I wrote in my journal note book about death and dying.

February 2, 1995

I had this terrible feeling inside like the one I get when I totally clean off my desk. I worry something will happen to me if I clean off my desk. It is weird that I bounce back and forth between wanting to die and being scared of dying, I am afraid of dying and living. I needed to get out of my head.

You know sometimes, I want my mom to make everything better by cleaning my apartment, doing my laundry and taking care of me when I am so sick. Yet, I do not want that on the other hand because I would have to have to sacrifice that since I do not want her downing me, making cuts on my husband, calling Betty lazy, and what I have told her.

I have never talked about Kathy's death because I did not want to be out of control of what I say since Mom often times misinterprets things. I guess I am lonely for the Mother that I would like to have.

Love,
Nancy

Chapter Thirteen

In March 1995, the psychiatrist told me that I needed to go into the hospital because he needed to put me on some different medication, but I refused.

Finally, I became unable to work. I got to the point when I would not even call into work until later in the day. I was really exhausted at work. My supervisor had quit and I was left by myself. I had to endure being by myself for three months. I talked to my new supervisor about my situation, and she said that if the doctor wanted me to go into the hospital then, I should go and that she would hold my spot for me when I got better, so I agreed to go in to the hospital in March 1995.

My first day there I cried and cried because I had heard horror stories about hospital visits from clients. Also, I was not open about my disability and had not come out of the closet yet. Fortunately, my insurance let me go into a hospital in another city to avoid running into any of my clients. The hospital was really nice. They had two floors one was high risk, and the other one let a patient go into the rest of the hospital. So that meant Nick could bring food to me when he came for a visit. Also, it had a patio and basketball court with a swing on it that made it nice for family visits.

Nick decided that he wanted his family to take care of Betty while I was in the hospital. They flew up and took her back with them. Then, when I got out of the hospital they brought her back. I do not know why Nick sent Betty to stay with his family when my family could have taken her to their house, so I could have seen her. I missed Betty really bad.

March 1995

I am feeling confused about how I feel. I don't feel sadness exactly. I cannot even cry when I think about Kathy my friend who committed suicide in 1994. I even figured out how I would do it. It frightens me that I have figured out two ways in case I have a bad day and decide to kill myself.

Love,
Nancy

At that time Betty was about one and a half years old. I missed her terribly. When I got out of the hospital, I had to take off work until August 1995. I did not know what to do with my time. So I slept a great deal of the time. I also spent time watching Betty.

In May of 1995, I became suicidal. The doctor put me back into the hospital. She said it worried her that I believed my family would be better off without me, and that Betty could have a better mom than I. I hate myself. This time in the hospital the doctor ordered that my parents come in for a conference. The social worker who called my mom said that if only one of my parents could attend, they wanted it to be Mom. When my parents came, my mom came expecting them to answer questions about my illness. However, it turned out awful. The social worker told my mom that it was her fault because she kept telling me that I needed to go back to work for everything to be OK.

The meeting was a disaster. I did not know what I needed, and they did not know how to help me. My relationship with Mom got strained.

I began to think that Mom was trying to take Betty away from me. It was part of my paranoia. Because I loved my parents, I just wanted them to understand what I was going through, and accept me for who I was which was a person with a mental illness, a thought disorder. There was a lot I did not understand even though I had been working with people with mental illnesses for three years. I did not know much, but I knew I was a sick person.

Nick and I moved into a much nicer apartment in July 1995. I was off work, so I had plenty of time to unpack.

I went back to work from 10:00 a.m. until 2:00p.m. Monday through Friday in August of 1995.

In July of 1995, Nick and I took a vacation to his home town. While I was there, I interviewed for a job at the same place I had worked before we moved from his home town in 1992. I was offered a job as the supervisor over the kitchen unit. I had a hard time deciding what to do. I really was not crazy about the job because I am not good at the kitchen.

My therapist had recommended that Nick and I move because of my negative relationship I had with my mom. In August 1995, Nick and I were lying in bed trying to decide whether or not to move back to Nick's home town or not because I was still struggling with my relationship with Mom. I was angry that my mental illness was interfering with my life. I told God it was not fair that I had to base my decisions of where I wanted to raise my child and make decisions around my mental illness. So I got angry and decided that I would just go and take all of my medications.

Nick held me down in bed until I had calmed down. Then, he made me call my therapist. She had me go to the hospital where I had been twice.

Nick had taken some allergy medicine and did not feel comfortable driving me there, so I called my dad and he took me to the hospital. By this time it was 1:00 a.m. Dad said that he wanted to stay until I was admitted. So, he sat with me until about 5 a.m. when I was admitted. It was a good thing because the Emergency Room was very busy and they needed someone to stay with me. The hospital did not check with my insurance company to determine if it were on their list. Even though the hospital was not on my insurance, the insurance had approved for me to go there so that I would not run into any of my clients, but later that morning the hospital sent me to a private hospital.

I had not come out of the closet yet to people that I had a mental illness and did not come out until 2004. I hated the private hospital. I had to walk through locked door after locked door. I called Nick and begged him to come get me, but he refused. Also, there was not enough room for everybody to sit in the television room.

I went in on Friday, so I had to wait until Monday to talk to the doctor. I swore to the doctor that I would never do it again if he would just let me out. I had been working part time and I called my coworker and told him I had to take Monday off. I did not figure it was any of his business as to why I had to take off work. So, after a quick visit in the hospital on the week end, I went back to work on Tuesday still working part time.

CHAPTER FOURTEEN

Betty had just turned two years old in August, and in September 1995 Nick and I decided to move back to his home town. I went back to work at the mental health center were I had spent that great year of my life between college and getting married the best year of my life. Working was hard for me because I had not worked full time since March 1995, and I was not ready to go back to work plus as I said earlier, "I was miserable because I hated working in the kitchen," and I hated working with one of the consumers. She was bossy and said things I disagreed with. On top of it all, my supervisor was not supportive at all. I was failing miserably, and I had to take a week off in November 1995 because I was so anxious that I could not get out the front door.

When we first moved, I had to find a psychiatrist and a therapist. The first therapist told me that she did not work with patients who had mental illnesses, but that another psychologist in her office did, so I began working with Dr. Kingsley. I was not for sure about my psychiatrist. She took me off all my medicines, and I felt great the first three weeks, then, I crashed and burned.

When Nick and I moved, we stayed with Nick's parents for about six weeks. Then, we rented a house. Then, my symptoms got worse. I began to feel sorry for myself, and here is what I wrote in October 1995.

October 13, 1995

I know I should look forward to the positive things in my life like Betty taking her first steps this weekend, the rest of my friends, family, and Nick going back to work tomorrow after being off for a month, but those good feelings have a hard time out weighing the dread I feel inside. I just keep asking God what I have done to deserve this. Why does He not make things better?

Love,
Nancy

CHAPTER FIFTEEN

Nick, Betty, and I flew up to my parents' home for Christmas 1995 to be with my family. While we were at my parents' house, I cried and cried. At that time, I told Nick that I needed to take off work again. However, he was not happy about it. He told me I should have told him that before we moved into that rental house. I tried to explain that I was trying my hardest, but I just could not do it anymore.

I had packed my mom's Christmas present in my suite case, but, it got broken on the way to my parents. My dad glued it back together for me, but I still feel guilty to this day.

I was so depressed that I did not feel anything. I felt numb. When we returned home from our trip, I realized I could go into the garage and kill myself with carbon monoxide poisoning, so I called my therapist and told him I needed to go to the hospital for my suicidal thoughts. He called the hospital. When I called Nick, he had his Mom come and stay with me until he could get home to take me to the hospital.

I spent my birthday in the hospital. The staff brought me a cup cake with a tooth pick with the plastic on the end that they lit up. While I was there, I learned about chair aerobics and the use of rubber bands. My favorite group was art. After my stay in the hospital, I went to day treatment for five months.

Following are some notes that I put in my journal while in the hospital:

January 7, 1996.

Today is an ok day. OK meaning I am not having a crisis. Although I am worried about leaving here. I am still afraid I might kill myself unless I am better. That is one thing I plan on being is better before I leave. I feel sort of anxious, but not where I feel physically sick.

Love,
Nancy

January 8, 1996

Today, I woke up wanting to die or at least thinking about it. I know I have reasons to live such as Betty and Nick, but also I have a reason for dying. I am so miserable inside that I cannot stand it. I know with this new therapy my therapist and another staff member want me to try that I may get better. I need to rethink my thoughts, and say something like, I know I am miserable now, but it won't last forever. But when I was thinking about dying I was wondering where I would be buried and where the funeral would be. Maybe, I can leave specific instructions with Nick that I want my funeral in my home town because that is really where all of my friends and family are. You know, I wonder if Kathy went through all of these thoughts before she killed herself. Maye if she had, she would not have killed herself. Maybe she would have gotten help. The thought of how she felt overburdened me. I pray that this is God's answer to my prayer. It is just that I feel defeated because the hospital should be considered as a last resort. Maybe, it was chosen to tell me that God heals in different ways and is the best for me.

January 9, 1996

This evening I talked to Mom on the phone when she called me. I am still in the hospital. She wanted to know if Nick and I were going to get a divorce. What a question! She said that Nick said that we were arguing when we were home for our Christmas visit. She blames Nick for my problems. I am tempted to kill myself. Then, I will not have to put up with her any more. Actually, she is not worth my killing myself, but I could still call her and tell her I do not want to talk to her any more unless she does not talk about my relationship with Nick. I think that is the only thing I can do to stop her from hurting me.

I think I am ready to go home. Maybe, it is so I can kill myself, but I do not know. I can only find out by leaving. I cannot hurt Nick and Betty by killing myself. I owe it to them to try some more. Without having to work, it makes it easier or perhaps bearable. I have not been that anxious today either, so this is good. There is a new girl here today who attempted suicide. We have a lot of emotions in common. We have been sitting here thinking and talking about how hopeless we both felt. It is nice to know that there is someone else who feels and really understands how I feel about dying.

Love,
Nancy

Before the days of no smoking in the hospital, patients were given two cigarettes a piece by the staff to smoke in the smoke room, so the patients begged me to tell the staff that I had started smoking, so the patients could smoke the two that I got. However, I did not know that the staff had to light up your cigarettes before going to the smoke room. Therefore, I gave it a shot, and boy was it nasty. I never did that again.

I began seeing a new doctor while I was in the hospital.

January 11, 1996

I have decided to apply for Social Security Disability Income. I know it is kind of degrading and people may see me as lazy or not trying. It is a hard decision to make. But my thoughts behind it are that I need time to get better. I managed working some, but I never got well. I was on survival mode. Well, I want more than that. I want to be alive. I want to enjoy living. And for right now I am just not able to work and do the house work and take care of Betty. I think I need to admit that that is OK. I guess I need to learn to accept myself and my situation-illness. Right now, I am scared about going home. I am afraid I will kill myself. I do not know what sparked Kathy to kill herself. A bad day at work, feeling physically ill, or the flat tire she had the week before. I do not think she planned it though I think she had something happen that morning, and she just decided she could not handle anything else. That is the way I feel right now. I guess I need to learn that it is OK to take off work which does not make me a bad person. I need to say that over and over and over again to myself. I need to allow myself to be ill and stop feeling guilty for it.

Love,
Nancy

January 12, 1996

Today, I woke up wanting to die or at least thinking about it. I know I have reasons to live such as Betty and Nick, but I, also have a reason for dying. I am so miserable inside that I cannot stand it. I know with this new therapy my therapist wants me to try that I need to rethink my thought and say something else like I know I am miserable now, but it won't last forever. But when I was thinking about dying, the same thoughts went through my mind as they did on January 9. Perhaps, this is the answer to my prayer. It is just I feel defeat. I just view myself as a failure. Now to rethink my view it could be said going into the hospital is the option that I chose to get better the fastest. I am so sleepy today. Yesterday, I took a one and a half hour nap and then, a four hour nap and still slept all night long. I think it might be the medicine because it can make one sleepy. I guess I will try and go to bed while I am able to sleep. I am actually seeing the paper cross eyed because my vision is so off focus. That is right the medicine also blurred my vision a great deal, so now I really cannot see the lines I am writing on unless I cross my eyes and then, I can see. Oh the joys of medicine.

One thing I will say is that the staff here are really wonderful. They are so sincere. I think I would like to work at a place like this which was the hospital I was in, so maybe, when I go back to work, I can apply to work at a place like this. I can apply at another place like this or maybe a residential setting. But for now I just want to get better. I mean I want to get better. I mean I want to get well enough to go back to work, so I do not want to kill myself but I want to enjoy life again. Once, I am stable and enjoying life then, let me try working again. That is if I live long enough.

I am scared that people won't support me. My therapist and Nick say they will support my decision. Nick even called a friend about hiring a lawyer who will only get paid if he wins my case and I get back pay. I wonder how many months I would get back pay. I am not looking to make a profit just enough to pay the bills.

I know that people say that I am really not as bad as I think I am but I think they just do not know how much my thinking is effected by my illness, my depression, and my voices. Also, my medication makes me feel drugged up and makes me have a flat affect. I cannot live with the medicines and I cannot live without them, so that makes me not feel like living. I will say this, I tried to suffocate myself in my pillow here at the hospital. Maybe drowning myself is not such a bad idea. At least, I could not change my mind. Hopefully, it would be fast and easy since I am not into pain.

I called Nick a few minutes ago, and he said, "I might not be able to come visit you because life goes on." In other words, he has more important things to do than to come and see me. It, also bothered me that he would not have my funeral in my hometown because I asked him to. I do not mind him burying me where we are living because he said that he wanted a place where Betty could come visit my grave site. He, also, said that he does not care what Mom and my family think. Now that kind of made me more than a little mad.

Love,
Nancy

That January 1996, while I was in the hospital, I applied for Social Security Disability Income. I had my interview over the phone. I, also, had a lady from the place where I had worked who helped me fill out the application. By the grace of God, my application was approved and I received my first check five months later in May 1996.

My SSDI was predated to September 1995 when I changed jobs because I was considered unable to work.

Prior to my taking off from work, I called my supervisor and told her that I needed to take off a year. She said that they would probably just fire me. She showed no sympathy or empathy for me. That saddened me because you would think that a mental health agency would have more sympathy and understanding. The CEO ended up approving my leave of absence. While I was off work, Betty went to day care. One day I talked to the lady in charge about how I had been suicidal, so she called Nick's mom to come get Betty. Years later, that lady became my ex-husband's mother in law. She is the sweetest lady. We greet each other with a hug. Her daughter, who is my children's step mother, is awesome too. She takes care of my kids like they are her own.

We, also, moved in to Nick's grandmother's house and rented it from his dad who had bought it for us to rent from him. While I was taking day treatment, I slept in my clothes and wore them the next day. I did not realize how wrinkled my clothes were and how sloppy I looked until I looked into the mirror one day.

Chapter Sixteen

SSDI, Social Security Disability Income, paid me $4,000.00 back pay which Nick and I wasted. I asked Nick if we could pay my parents the $1400.00 we owed for moving us in September 1992, but Nick said "No". He used it all up on yard work and buying a used car.

In May 1996, On Mother's Day weekend, I got really angry at Nick for something that I do not remember for what. I decided to off myself by taking all of my medicine. Then, I got to thinking about what Betty would do without me, so I called my psychiatrist and he insisted that I come by ambulance, but we only lived across the street from the hospital. I could just imagine the ambulance, police, and fireman coming to my house. Then, I promised I would get someone to bring me to the hospital, so I called Nick and told him that my doctor wanted me to go to the hospital. So one of Nick's friends took me to the hospital.

After they pumped my stomach that made me sick, a nurse had the gall to ask me if I were sure that I had taken my medicine because they could not find anything in my stomach. Well, it was six hours after I had arrived at the emergency room before they pumped my stomach.

I did not tell Nick what I had done until five days later. I begged him not to tell his parents or anyone else. I do not know if he ever did, but when we went to court, Nick's lawyer said that I was violent because I had attempted suicide. In the past, I had tried to kill myself by drowning myself and suffocating myself at the hospital.

I do think Nick never trusted me again. I, also, did not tell my family for years that I had attempted suicide because I was worried they would always be expecting me to kill myself, so now when I tell my dad that I need to go to the hospital, he knows I need to go.

March 6, 1996

Today, I am writing because I feel suicidal. I feel like going and killing myself. I have been thinking about it for several days. Today, is worse though. I just feel hopeless again, so I decided to write about it. My throat hurts today too. I promised Lori that I would come in tomorrow, so I feel like I should at least make that commitment. I would hate for her to feel guilty if I did something. But, hopefully people would realize I have to take responsibility for myself and my own actions.

Well, I have just about made it through the evening. I am about to go to bed. Nick just came in and said to me as I was lying in bed, "If you are going to go to bed, then, you need to turn the TV and lights off." When I said, "You leave the TV on in the morning." Nick said, "Excuse the heck out of me." That was not really deserved if you ask me.

Right now I am worried about what people will think of me when I am dead. Like what would people think if they read my journals? I would have no control over them. Although, I have given Nick instructions to burn my journals when I die, but I doubt he will. I wonder what he will do when I do die. I have asked him before if he would remarry, and he said that he would not. My first doctor after we moved once told me that step families are not good, and that is why I should not kill myself. Like I told Lula today, "I have reasons to live who are Nick and Betty, but I, also, have a reason to die- depression." I just feel so hopeless. It seems like change is always occurring. Change scares me. I am afraid of the unknown. I am afraid of dying because I do not know if I would go to heaven or hell if I killed myself. I wonder what Kathy thought when she was killing herself. I wonder what she is doing tonight. Is she in heaven or hell? I used to know what I believed that she was in heaven, but now, I do not know any more. I feel kind of lost.

Love,

Nancy

After I finished my day treatment at the hospital in May 1996, I needed to find something to do. Therefore, I contacted an office that helps the mentally Ill's Family Members, and I began volunteering in May 1996. There were days when I was so sleepy from the medication that I was on that I would leave and return in the afternoon. That office was a place where I could go, feel at peace, and be able to share my story. The year that I volunteered at that office, I met some good friends. One was the children's advocate and the other the office manager.

I had not come out of the closet yet about my having Schizoaffective Disorder. I felt so misunderstood especially around family and ex in-laws. I wrote an article for the newsletter that was published quarterly about how my children had been taken away from me by Nick's parents while I was in the hospital.

That December 1996, on Christmas Day I told Nick I thought I was pregnant. The birth control we used failed us, so I went to a drug store, the only store open, and bought a pregnancy test and sure enough I was pregnant. That was a great Christmas.

When we told Nick's parents, they became really upset. Nick's mom asked me if I thought about how I was going to take care of a baby when I could not take care of Betty. I told her that I did not know, but that all I could do was to try. We tried to explain to them about how the birth control had failed us, but that did not help any. Then, Nick's sister whose husband is a pharmacist got in the picture and informed me that I would have to go without my medicine. She was really critical. I think it was because they were not able to have children, so they adopted a baby girl in 1997 and later a baby boy.

One day when I went to my doctor and my therapist, my doctor increased my medicine to 20mg. He thought I should see my therapist. I told him I did not think it would help. I have been getting suicidal since January 1995. I am tired of hearing voices telling me to kill myself. Sometimes, I think it is God who wants me dead because I keep hearing those terrible voices. Nick hid my medicine, but he cannot keep me from driving.

My doctor asked me if I would be willing to go to the hospital if I got worse. I did not want to go because I am scared. I do not want to die but at the same time my voices want me to die. I do not understand why they want me to die because then they would die. My therapist told me my voices are not real, but they seem real to me. I, also, have been getting confused like my brain stops processing. I, also, feel fake and not real that is a bad feeling. When Nick is home, I lay in bed because the voices and anxiety subside.

One day, I told Nick I wanted to take a nap and that it was up to him to watch Betty. When I woke up from my nap, Nick had fallen asleep, and left Betty to do what she wanted to do. I looked and was amazed. Betty had gotten into my red fingernail polish and painted her body and her bedding.

Mom called and said that she saw this coming because I read two books on anxiety. She said that I am just feeling sorry for myself. She just does not understand. I am glad she is not my therapist. Perhaps, I have given up on living. I do not know how to dream. Nick is always coming up with something to dream about: a boat, football season tickets, and so on.

You would think that I would look forward to having this baby. But so far, I just cannot get past the fear of having to take care of a baby when he or she is born.

My therapist asked me if I really wanted this baby. I told him that I did, but I am just scared. My doctor does not know why I get this way. Mom said that it is all my fault. She, also, blamed Nick for making the house dirty and for getting us in financial trouble when we got married. I told her that I did not talk about Dad and she should not talk about Nick. But she kept on talking about Nick. She told me to make a cleaning schedule with Nick. Dad does not help mom, so why should Nick help me? Mom helps me some times but when I am hearing that little man in my head telling me to kill myself, her comments do not help. Mom is just clueless. She told me just to tell that little man to leave me alone, but he does not listen to me. Sometimes, I just feel like I am not real.

Mom called again to apologize to me. I told her that she hurt my feelings, and that she does not understand. **She does not understand**. She said that she understands more than I think she does.

When I told my psychiatrist I was pregnant, he told me to go off all my medicine.

Then, when I went to the OBGYN, he told me to go back on my medication because he had learned that women on these medications needed to be on them for a reason. He, also, told me that there was no proof that the medication I was on would have any side effects on my unborn child. I never told anyone except my family that I stayed on my medications and until this day I do not know if Nick ever told his family.

My pregnancy went well until almost the end when I got sick with vomiting. I could not even keep water down, so on a Monday in July 1997, I went to the OBGYN. I had lost eight pounds over the weekend. I ended up being hospitalized for a week because I was dehydrated. Then, the doctor decided to do a scope of my esophagus. He discovered that I have GERD, Gastro Esophageal Reflux Disease.

Nick called my parents and told them that Andrew was going to be born soon. Mom and Dad drove down, but the doctor said he wanted to prolong my pregnancy closer to due date which was Betty's birthday. After hearing that news, Mom and Dad returned home.

Then, on August 15, 1997, Andrew was born. He weighed a whopping 9 pounds and 15 ounces. When Andrew was born, he did not respond to the nurse giving him a shot. Before I even got to hold Andrew, the hospital took Andrew away from me to a hospital that had a Neonatal Intensive Care Unit. Andrew looked funny because he was so big compared to those tiny preemies. The doctors ran all kinds of tests on him, and they came to the conclusion that Andrew had withdrawal symptoms from the medications that I had been taking.

Today, Andrew is a football player and soccer player for his high school, and makes A's and B's in school. Nothing wrong with him. I am glad that I stayed on my medicine despite that Nick's sister insisted that I quit taking it. My symptoms were already bad even on medicine. I can only imagine what I would have gone through without them.

My parents came down with the intention that Mom stay three weeks, but she just kept harping over Nick. I could not tell her all the things that were going on in my life because it would have made things worse.

On the day that Dad and I went to get Andrew from the hospital, we went to the store to get formula. While we were in the store, Nick came and parked so close to our car that my Dad could not get in it. When he finally came to the car, he told us that he wanted to go with us, and he wanted to make sure that we did not go without him.

About two days after Andrew was dismissed from the hospital, Dad went home. When Nick wasn't home, Mom just kept on harping about Nick. It got so bad that I finally could not take it anymore. I told Mom that if she could not stop complaining then she would need to leave. The next day she flew home.

Our Sunday school class took turns bringing us meals which we greatly appreciated. My favorite meal was green pea soup. I asked my friend for her recipe and she said that she just followed the recipe on the package. Whatever she did it was good.

Andrew was not like Betty who started sleeping through the night at the age of two weeks. Betty would sleep, eat, and sleep some more. Andrew stayed awake most of the day and night. He required more care than Betty. While Mom was with me, she helped with cleaning the house which she always did. At that time, Nick did not help with cleaning. Matter of fact, he would drag out all kinds of stuff. I think it was a way of keeping control of things. I did my best to try and take care of Betty and

Andrew, but it was a real struggle. Nick would not get up with Andrew even on the nights when he did not have to get up the next morning which left me to take care of him by myself.

I was on some very strong medicine. If I remember right, I was on about eleven different psychiatric meds. This made it hard for me to wake up long enough to take care of Andrew in the middle of the night. My brother once said to me he could understand why I was not hungry for breakfast because I was still full from the previous night's medicine.

My doctor finally told me that my trying was not good enough anymore and that I needed to be in the hospital. By this time, he had moved his office. Therefore, I had to go into another hospital where I stayed about a week. By this time, it was October. I came home from the hospital still not feeling well. I came home and tried to take care of Andrew and Betty. One night Andrew was crying so, I got up. I was so confused and could not figure out what to do. He needed to be fed, but all I could seem to do was try and feed him with a bottle of deodorant that was sitting on the edge of the bed. I finally got up and went back to bed with Andrew still crying. Nick finally yelled at me to go get the formula and make him a bottle. Well, I could not do it because I was too confused. Then, he yelled at me to go to bed and he would feed him.

The next day, Betty woke up with vomiting, and I was left at home to take care of her. The hospital called me to see why I had not come in for day treatment. I explained to them what was going on. They had me call Nick to come home from work to take care of Betty because I needed to be in the hospital. Then, I drove myself to the hospital which was a forty minute drive and, I was readmitted to the hospital.

While I was attending the hospital which I had five different visits in six months the staff was shocked because Nick did "drive by drop offs". The nurses called me a "drive by drop off" patient because Nick would drive me to the emergency room and leave me at the door. A few days later. Nick told me that he had to take Betty to the hospital because she was dehydrated. By this time, it was Halloween. So, Betty who was four spent Halloween in the hospital. I felt really guilty because I could not take her trick or treating.

October 30, 1997

Today was awful. I got so confused that I called the nurses two times and I do not remember the rest of the day. I was so confused that I finally called Nick at work and asked him to come home. Then, I was really angry when Teri, a nurse, said that she would call Department Human Services if Nick and his parents did not come in for a family meeting with Louis, the social worker. I do not want a family meeting with Nick's parents.

Love,
Nancy

October 31, 1997

Right now I am worried about Betty and Andrew. I called Jackie, my baby sitter, and asked her about Betty. She told me Betty is with Nick's mom right now. But I want to go home. This is like a nightmare that is coming to me. I am angry that I am not able to take care of my kids. I am anxious about having a meeting with Louis, Nick's parents, Nick, my doctor, and myself about my ability to take care of Betty and Andrew. Once, they know I am afraid of them, I do not know what will be said. I am scared of what will happen if I cannot take care of Andrew and Betty.

This really scares me. I feel so guilty. I feel like I have let people down especially Mom, Dad, and Nick's parents and Nick.

Love,
Nancy

In November 1997, my psychiatrist and the social worker called a meeting with Nick and his parents. They said that if the family did not come in for a meeting then, they were going to call Child Protective Services, so his parents grudgingly went in for a conference. At that point my doctor and the social worker said that I could not be left alone with my children because I might unintentionally hurt them. So it was decided that Betty and Andrew would go to live with Nick's parents.

Nick would not take me to see the children. I remember sitting on the couch screaming out to God. "Why is this happening to me?" That was the first worst day in my life. I never wanted to hurt my children nor did I ever try to hurt them. So, Nick requested that the doctor write a letter stating that I could not be left alone with the children until I was better. Nick said that he needed the letter in case one of the kids needed medical care. That letter came back to haunt me.

We went to court several times to try and get that removed but today in 2014 I still have to have supervised visits with Andrew. Betty is old enough that I can now have her by herself. My supervision just means that Dad or another adult has to be with me when I am with Andrew. However, Nick said after Andrew turned sixteen that I could be with him by myself, but my dad continues to be with me when I am with him. We get to spend the night with Betty and Andrew. I never have told my children that I have to have an adult with me when I am with them.

I continued to be hospitalized once in November 1997 and once in December 1997. During one of my visitations to the hospital, I was walking down the hall and saw a mattress out in the hall. There were two cleaning ladies working in a room and I remember thinking to myself why did they put the mattress in the hall? When I got to my room I realized it was my mattress. I called Nick and told him that my mattress was in the hall he told me I was hallucinating and for me to get the nurse, and she confirmed what I had told him. She said that was because they could not keep me out of bed. I could not stay awake because I was on so much medication that it caused me to sleep on the couch during group in the group room. To this date when I go to the hospital, I worry I will get in trouble for sleeping during groups. During my hospital visits, I was told, "You are adults, and you can get up on your own."

During my hospital visit in January 1998, Nick decided that the hospital was not doing a good enough job with me, so he arranged to take me to a hospital in another city which was about an hour and forty five minutes' drive. It was supposed to be a Christian based provider. When he moved me, he did not tell my parents where he was taking me.

My parents had no clue where I was because Nick had mentioned that he had investigated a place in another state that had long term care for mentally ill patients. Mom said they sat down and cried because they did not know what had happened to me. Finally, I was able enough to call them and tell them where I was. My parents and my sister flew down and stayed for the week end in a hotel and came for visits during visitation. But Nick would not come visit me while I was there about ten days.

The facility was pretty nice. We had chapel services on a daily basis or I guess they were more like Bible studies. They, also, had a time for the relatives to come to a meeting for recovery, so my mom, Dad and, my sister came to the meetings. I think it is sad that my family came from 700 miles away when Nick would not come the short drive which was about 120 miles. He did not even come when my family came. It was a time of great pain for me. Nick wanted the hospital to keep me for three months or so. But because insurance companies limited the length of time that a patient could stay in the hospital, I was released after ten days and went home.

Because my children were living with Nick's parents, I did not get to see them. I had asked Nick to bring my children to the hospital to see me, but he said that he was too busy. When Nick and I arrived home after being released from the hospital, I begged Nick to take me to see Betty and Andrew who were at his parents' house, but he would not do that for me.

When I got home, I realized that Nick had packed all of my ceramic pig collection in containers. He had, also, taken all our wedding pictures off the walls. But I was so out of it that I did not see anything wrong about it.

In February of 1998, because I was trying to stay out of the hospital, Dad came to stay with me for a week. However, it did not work, and I ended up in the hospital anyway.

At this time Nick's dad, took my dad to a nice restaurant for breakfast. He told my dad that he thought that Nick could not take care of the two children by himself. He, also, said that Nick's sister could adopt Betty, but that someone else would have to take Andrew.

My parents talked to my sister, and she said that she could take both Betty and Andrew until I could get better.

Also, Nick's dad tried to get me to take Electric Shock Treatment, ECT, but I refused because I knew people who had it and they had lost memory. I did not want to take the chance of losing the memories of Betty and Andrew. To this day, I still refuse ECT unless I am ordered by a judge. Nick's father told me that his own mother had ECT and it was successful. It was at this time that Nick's dad told me and my dad that Nick could not take care of the kids on his own.

In March 1998, I was back in the hospital. On March 17, 1998 Nick came to the hospital for a quick thirty minute visit. About thirty minutes later the sheriffs' deputies came and delivered divorce papers to me. I never saw it coming. Nick never mentioned to me that he was divorcing me. He said that I just forgot that he told me. However, I know I would not have forgotten news like that even though I was messed up very badly. I was devastated.

I couldn't believe what was happening to me. I had lost custody of my children and now the man that I leaned on had abandoned me in the hospital. Nick did not bring Betty and Andrew up to see me while I was in the hospital where I had been so many times. He said that he was too busy.

Some people today think he is a coward for the way he treated me. I asked Nick at a later date if he regretted divorcing me like he did and he said, "No, I had to choose between taking care of you and taking care of the kids, and I chose to take care of the kids." I had been very dependent on Nick. No matter how abusive he was, I still loved him, and I just did not understand why he was divorcing me.

Mom taped my conversation that I had with her the night I got my divorce papers, and how sad I was. In the end, I was better off without Nick. The only thing I regret was not taking the kids and leaving Nick first.

Because Mom and Dad lived in another state, when I called and told them the news about my divorce, they had to find a lawyer for me very quickly. Because they did not know any attorneys my dad called one of the national organizations in which he was a member, and asked them if they knew of any lawyers in the state in which I was living. The attorney that was recommended was not available, but the person who answered the phone recommended one of the other attorneys in the office. Therefore, my parents got my first lawyer, Mr. Jones. When Mr. Jones came to the hospital to see me, he asked me if I understood what was going on, I assured him I did.

In the meantime Mom and Dad drove down and picked me up from the hospital on March 20, 1998. We went to Mr. Jones's office where he asked me if I wanted to be declared incompetent and stop the divorce because in that state a spouse cannot divorce the other spouse if that spouse is mentally ill. I told him, "No." because I knew that if I were declared incompetent that I would have a very difficult time getting my rights back and being able to make decisions concerning my finances and any legal issues. If I had not known these facts I might have let the courts declare me incompetent.

I had volunteered in the office for the families of the mentally Ill. When I told the state appointed children's advocate about my parents having to come, she invited us to stay in her house. We had a court date set for nine days after I got my divorce papers.

Nick had it set in his mind that I could only see my children for four hours from the time the divorce papers were delivered to me and the first court date and never see them again. However, when the first hearing was held, I was under so much medication that my mind could not function properly, and my attorney advised me not to go to court, but let the children's advocate and my parents represent me. The judge ruled that I could see Betty and Andrew for four hours before I left the city. The day came when I was able to see my children for the last time before I left. I remember playing Candy Land with Betty and holding Andrew. Nick came to unlock the door because he had already changed the locks, but the judge had ordered him not to be in the house with me while I was there, so he and his dad sat outside in his car in the next door neighbor's driveway. I was allowed to gather some of my belongings. Some of them were my journals, but the journals could not be found in the house. Evidently, Nick had given them to his attorney without my knowledge, because they later showed up in court where my private most intimate thoughts were exposed. Also, he had put all my clothes in a car that he said that I could have.

The judge ordered that the journals be returned to me when he handed down the final decision in November. Because I felt what I had written my feelings at that particular time of my life, and it caused me to lose the custody of my children, I did not journal for years after that incident.

At the end of the four hours, Nick came back into the house and I had to say goodbye to my children. Then, came the second worst day in my life not knowing if I would only be able to see my children once a month until November, then not ever see them again.

Mom told me that when we left that I started talking about all of the abuse that I had experienced. She understood that I could not talk about it with her while I was living with Nick because if I had there would have been consequences.

Chapter Seventeen

———— ⤬ ————

On April 9, 1998, my mom's birthday, I started treatment at the local mental health center. I began going to four groups a week and one time a week for individual therapy. My favorite group was art therapy that allowed me to express my feelings, and boy did I have feelings. I was hurt over my marriage and experienced grief over not being able to see my children. I was scared, confused, and embarrassed. I stayed in therapy for about three years at one of the mental health counseling services located in the area where I live.

In July 1998, I went to a local crisis center for the first time. The crisis center is for people who really do not need to be hospitalized but could use some intense therapy. It is a big house that holds up to seven residents at a time. The bill was based on the individual's income, and I only had to pay $14.00 a day.

At that time, they had a cat there, and I fell in love with the cat. So after my stay, I asked my mom if I could get a cat, and she agreed. I got my cat in July 1998. I named her Hope because she brought some purpose into my life. Unfortunately for me Hope would only sit in my mom's lap. She would come rub her head on my dad's and my feet.

When my mom passed away, Hope finally started sitting in my lap. Mom always said that Hope knew who fed her, and that is why she sat in my mom's lap because my mom took care of her needs.

Before I moved back to my parents, I spent most of my time in bed because I did not have anything to do, and I was extremely over medicated. I, also, missed Betty and Andrew because they were staying with Nick's parents. Once I moved in with my parents they would not let me sleep all day.

I started going to a mission based group of ladies who took turns reading a book a month. These ladies took me under their wings and prayed for me. They even purchased clothing for my children for Christmas.

At the time I moved back in with my mom and my dad, they were teaching in the adult education program for the public schools. They got me started volunteering with them. I struggled with my hallucinations, but I eventually learned coping skills from therapy.

When I moved back in with my mom and my dad, I had the same room that Nick and I had while we stayed there in 1993-1994. However, I did not see it as the dungeon because it was private and outside the family room with an outside entrance.

Mom was so bitter about my divorce that all she could do was talk about what abuse Nick had done to me and what a bad person that he was. I think that she almost drove the rest of the family crazy talking about the situation because that is about the only thing she wanted to talk about with anyone.

My brother, Dad, Mom, and I went to court on Tuesday the week of Thanksgiving 1998 for the divorce hearing and had to return on Wednesday for the judge's decision to determine the custody of Betty and Andrew. Nick's attorney had a secretary who was a personal friend of Nick's family. Nick's attorney was, also, a good buddy with the judge.

I did not stand a chance, and I am sure that I was discriminated against because I was from another state. However, I was awarded supervised visitation twice a month. This was a huge relief to me because I knew that I at least could see my children two times a month. When it came to my supervision, the judge ordered the children's advocate as my supervisor. I had Betty and Andrew for forty eight hours a weekend for two weekends a month. I was, also, allowed to have my children one week for Spring Break and one week in the summer with the stipulation that I could not take them out of the state. However, Nick has been gracious enough to allow me to have them a week between Christmas and New Years for which I am very grateful.

The judge, also, allotted some things to me like Nick's computer that he had bought with money that was from a grant that I had gotten to further my education. But Nick said that he gave the printer away to his brother-in-law. Therefore, I was not awarded the printer.

Once again, we were allowed to go back into the house to get things like my china, crystal, silver ware, a CD player, and my journals which the judge ordered Nick to return to me. We had to take my love seat that my mom had purchased for me in 1991 with some of my other belongings to a storage unit until my brother and nephew could return at a later date and bring them home.

Because the decision was made late in the day, we had to drive all night in order for us to make it back home for Thanksgiving dinner.

That Thanksgiving all my mom could talk about was Nick and my divorce trial. The rest of the family told her if she could not stop talking about the trial and Nick that she needed to go be by herself, so she went to the basement to finish her meal.

I decided that day that I had to move out on my own. I did not have a car, therefore, I depended on borrowing my parents' car. I got a car in my divorce settlement, but I sold it to the next door neighbor for what we had purchased it for from them. I felt stuck.

I started looking for an apartment that next week. My mom went with me and we looked at some grungy places. At one of the apartments they charged extra for carpet in the entry way of the building. At those same apartments the water heaters were out in the open in the kitchen. Mom said that she considered calling the housing authority and reporting them. Then, one Sunday I saw an ad in the newspaper for an apartment that cost just $250.00 a month. I knew I could afford it because I did not have any bills coming out of my Social Security Disability Income check. I got Mom to go with me to look at it even though it was raining. The apartment was really nice and had one bedroom. The apartment manager approved my application and I moved in the apartment the day after Christmas 1998.

I knew God was with me on this move to independence because everything I purchased was on sale, and I had to start all over again.

My family told me I needed to get a job. The first place I got a job was an assembly plant for a company that made parts for an auto company. That job lasted two days.

Next, I got a job at a well-known store chain in March 1999. I worked ten hours a week in the jewelry department for three years.

During this time, I was going to visit my children every other weekend. My Supervisor was great about letting me take the weekends off to go see my children.

At the same time, I started volunteering for the adult education program with my mom and Dad. Then, the program director asked me if I wanted a paid position and I said, "Yes." Later on, the people in charge of me came and said that I had lost some things and that it be best if I resigned. However, there was another lady working with me who could have been losing the paper work.

CHAPTER EIGHTEEN

In 1999, a problem arose with the court appointed supervisor of my visitation. She was finding it harder and harder to plan her weekends free for my visits. The supervisor was working on her masters' degree, and her weekends got tied up. We went back to court to ask the judge, which was a different one than the one who had heard the divorce hearing, to let my mom and my dad be supervisors. No one would have predicted what the judge would order. She ordered that my mom and my dad would take turns with Nick's mom and dad each of them supervising once a month. For about two years, my parents took turns supervising the kids and me. It was tough on me staying at Nick's mom and dad's house. At night I could hear both of his parents locking their bedroom doors. They made me pay for the food for Betty, Andrew, and myself.

Because they would not come pick me up at the airport, sometimes I had to take a cab to their house. However, sometimes a friend would take me from the airport to Nick's parents' house, and afterwards, back to the airport or her house. Sometimes the court appointed supervisor would pick me up at the airport, take me to her home, then, and pick up the children for the week end. When the visitation was over, she would take me back to the airport. I finally started renting a car. Then, at least I was not stuck with nowhere to go between the time the visitation was over, and the time to return to the airport.

At first, when I started staying with Nick's parents, I did not go to church because I was still overly medicated and found it hard to get up in the morning to go to church. However, I finally started going. I remember my first visit to Sunday school. The welcome lady suggested I go to a certain class, but when I got in the class it was for married couples. So I ended up in a class for ladies of all ages, married, single, or divorced. This group of ladies welcomed me in the class. They loved me depressed, anxious and all. Unfortunately, over the last several years we have been driving to see my children. When we drive there, we have to leave early Sunday morning in order to return home by midnight.

I had stopped going to my home church for ten years because the Sunday school teacher in my class had made the comment that Christians experience depression because they are living in sin. After that, my mom and I stopped going to church.

We started staying at a motel about sixteen years ago, and until this day we stay in the same room when we go to see my children. The hotel has an indoor pool in which my kids learned to swim. Onetime, Andrew could not get in the water because he had an ear infection. He decided that he would jump in any ways. I was able to grab him out of the water without him getting his hair wet.

After staying with Nick's parents, we went back to court one last time to change the supervision. My psychiatrist did a deposition via satellite and even said that he would let me baby sit his children. The judge refused to listen to the deposition because Nick's attorney said that my doctor was self-serving and could not be trusted.

When we went to court, Nick's mom brought a journal that she had kept during my visits and, also, during the visits I had with my mom and my dad. I do not understand how she could journal about my visitation with my mom and my dad. After that court hearing, my parents told me that from then on they would go down with me every time, so I would not have to stay with Nick's mom and dad. I decided after that to just stick it out with my visitations until the children turn eighteen. That's a long time considering Betty was five years old, and Andrew was fifteen months old when I left my children after my divorce.

We began having birthday parties for Betty and Andrew when they were five and one year old. We would invite my friend Candy, and her son to the birthday parties. Of course, the court appointed supervisor was there. Because Betty and Andrew were involved in soccer when Betty was about six years old and Andrew was about four, we would, also, invite their team mates to their parties. However, we found that they did not come to our parties, so we stopped having the parties when they were about ten.

We always went to the kids' soccer games no matter what the weather. Come snow or beautiful weather, we toughed it out. I remember one time when it was snowing, and Mom and I had to buy coats to go to the game. I loved that coat and still have it to this day. Betty played about four or five years and Andrew played about three years.

Now Andrew likes to fish and hunt. Every year the week end before Thanksgiving Andrew, his father, and his step brother go hunting for some special occasion. Therefore, I have to plan my week ends around that period of time. Andrew is blessed with a great deal of patience when it comes to fishing. No matter where we go for our week long vacations, we always plan a day for Andrew to fish with my dad. My dad takes Andrew fishing, and Andrew's dad takes him hunting and fishing. During the Spring

Break, we stay at a ranch that has some fishing ponds, so he gets to go fishing every day.

By 2001, I was working two jobs, and my income was getting close to the maximum that I could earn outside of my Social Security Disability Income. Therefore, I decided to get a full time job. I interviewed for several places, and was finally hired for a position in June 2001 as an employment counselor and later moved to be a family counselor in an abused women's shelter. I did pretty well for the most part.

On April 28, 2002, I wrote Nick a letter. I wrote it to help get my feelings out, and never had any intention of mailing it to him. So here it is.

April 28, 2002

Dear Nick,

I really do not know where to start. I have so many feelings flowing to my heart that I feel over whelmed. The last few months have been really hard on me. But you know what? You may say hurtful things to me, but I am not going to relapse which is probably what you would like to see happen. However, I am stronger than you think, so this is where I'll begin.

For the last two and a half years, I have been staying with your mom and Dad once a month. I did not realize just how much they opposed me until your mom read the journal that your mom kept of my visits with them and even my visits with my parents. People are dumb founded when they hear that your mom and Dad charged me for the food for Betty, Andrew, and me. I do not mind paying them, but I have to ask, just how much for food do you pay to your parents when they have Betty and Andrew? Then, in the journal your mom wrote that she did not charge me for the quarter of a tank of gas she used when we went to see the Christmas lights in the park. The idea of charging me for the gas is simply ridiculous. I pay $240.00 for a plane ticket, $60.00 for the car rental, and spending money for Betty and Andrew. It is difficult for me to understand how your parents who are only out about $40.00, and they make a considerable more amount of money than I do would even consider the idea of my paying for food. They should want their grandchildren to have a good relationship with their mother. They need to admit that God has worked miracles in my life and that I am now capable of handling the children by myself. In your mom's journal she only noted the negative stuff but not about the positive stuff.

If any one of us has problems, I would say it is your parents and yourself. You should never have divorced me while I was in the hospital, and your dad would have not conceived the idea of adopting out Betty and Andrew and separating them. If your mom would have been more supportive of me during our marriage instead of being critical, she could have offered to help me clean the house because you would not help me either. I know that with your support I could have been able to keep Betty and Andrew in our home when we were married. You should not have abused me mentally, physically, emotionally, and sexually. I have only one regret in my life, and that is I did not take both children, and leave you before you divorced me.

I know I have said a lot of negative things about my mom. But you know what? My mom loves me and no matter what of all of the hateful things I have said and done my mom still loves me and will never leave me. Where were you when I needed you most? Out fishing is where you were. Instead of staying with me until I was admitted to the hospital you left me with "drive by drop offs." Even the staff at the hospital could not believe how unsupportive you were and still are.

As I said earlier, I have been through a lot these past few months. The biggest blow came when the judge dismissed my case of trying for unsupervised visits and visits in my home state. I am greatly hurt because I am better now and you cannot admit that. You are so blinded by Satan's sun glasses that you cannot admit that I could get better without you. The truth of the matter is that God has healed me. I do not look to relapse because God has healed me. As a Christian you should be happy for me that I have returned to work full time in the mental health profession and still working two part time jobs, with my new business in cosmetics. You should be supportive of me.

Sometimes, I want to call pastor Berry at the church and share with him how the secretary of your church, your mom, could treat someone like your parents have treated me. Your dad stayed in his room and watched TV instead of socializing. He did not have one positive thing to say to me except that I bought a Chevy Cavalier, and he has heard that it is a good car. Other than that, he has said negative things about my parenting skills even in front of Betty and Andrew. Your dad has strived to do the opposite.

In your mom's journal she wrote about spying on me at church and that I was confused and went to the wrong

Sunday school class which is where I was led to go by the welcome ladies at church. I was not confused because I realized as soon as I went there I was in the wrong class so I left and found the right one.

Your mom and dad's behavior brings me to a decision that you need to know. I am no longer going to be staying with your parents. My mom and my dad will be coming with me in the future. This has been a costly decision but I do not want to impose on your mom and dad for anything else. Because of this decision I am moving back in with my mom and my dad in May. I will be out of my apartment by June 1st. My mom and my dad are very close. They are very supportive of me and my decision to do what I have to do to see my children. I love Betty and Andrew with all of my heart. That is why I continue to go to the expense of my visitation with them.

I realize that you are pretty mad at me because I did not take the kids to their soccer games on Saturday. I made that decision with the kids in mind. Andrew was too sick to go and sit through Betty's game because he was running a temperature. Because of my having to be supervised, Mom and I could not split up and one of us keep Andrew in the hotel room and one of us go to Betty's game. You brought this on yourself when you would not agree for me to go off supervised visitation, so do not get mad at me. It is your fault. My attorney, also, told me that when it is my week end with Betty and Andrew I call the shots. If you do not like it then, you should have not divorced me because you could still be controlling me. But now you cannot control me. You can try and intimidate me, and sometimes you succeed. However, I am continuing to work on that very issue in therapy. I do not know how or when, but it will happen. God is blessing me with a good relationship with Betty and Andrew. Someday, they are going to come live with me. They may be eighteen, but God will bring them to live with me one day. I believe God has promised that I will have Betty and Andrew. It is just I am on God's time table and not my own. I look forward to the future.

Today, you made me mad when you insinuated that I am telling negative things to Betty about indoor soccer. You can try and get me to obey you, but you are in tough luck. I may be mad, but I am not going to relapse. You are just trying to control me, but you cannot. I will not say anything more at this point because I have already addressed this issue. Probably, one of the hardest things I do every day is to pray for you and your family. I would like to be able to reconcile our differences for the sake of the children. I do not want to get back with you because you have hurt me, and I believe that I am much better off without you being an intimate part of my life. But for the sake of the children I wish we could reconcile our differences and let me see the kids unsupervised where I live. I am not going to hurt the children. However, you continue to hurt Betty and Andrew because of the restrictions that you have placed on me. The kids have said that they would love to come to my home for a visit. My sister-in-law has never seen Andrew and my brother only saw Andrew when he was two years old when I was with my supervisor.

Nick, there are a lot of times when I have called you about every bad name that I can think of. Even my therapist asked me, "Is it just me, or is he really a jerk?" and I have to agree with her that you really are. You have hurt me beyond imagination. I pray to God to help me forgive you but that does not mean I will forget what you have done and continually do to me. However, I need to get some of this anger out that I have inside of me. It is not easy feeling this way. I loved you for a very long time. I am sorry I got sick, but I could not help it. You on the other hand could help your reaction to my illness.

The other day when we were in court, and your attorney asked me what I would do if the roles were reversed between you and me, I honestly could say that I would have not left you like you abandoned me in the hospital. You kicked me when I was down. Guess what? I am not down any more. God has healed me as I have already said in this letter. You can continue to choose to believe what you want about my condition, or you can choose the truth. Someday Betty and Andrew are going to see through you and you are going to regret having treated me like you did. You may try and separate me from Betty and Andrew, but you cannot take away the love that we share. God is on my side. I do not really understand why I lost my case, but God will be victorious, and He is victorious in my life now. You cannot take my faith away from me.

When I started praying for a full time job, I prayed that the Lord would use my life experiences for His glory and that is what has happened. I work with abused women in helping them get jobs or an education for which they are looking. It will be a year in June that I have been working fulltime. I know you are mad that I am working full time and that I am not on disability any more. The truth is you just want your money, and you do not like being paid less. God has healed me, and to that I am grateful. I truly believe that because we are divorced I am better because I do not have to deal with you. Now, I am better and I do not want you back, but as I said earlier I would like reconciliation, so we can both be the parents we want to be. Let us do it for Betty and Andrew. Surely, we can rise above our own issues and provide good parental care.

Well, I need to go now because I have said my peace.

Sincerely yours,

Nancy

In March 2004, my supervisor called me into her office and said that she had had complaints that I was sleeping while meeting with clients. She made me sign papers dating back to October 2003 stating that I was in trouble, and that I could either resign or be fired. At first, I wanted them to fire me, so I could collect unemployment. But then, I decided I would step out into a leap of faith and give a four week notice. I went to the personal care home for adults who had mental illnesses. The lady in charge had hired me in 1993 to work at a club house program which was the last job I had at the mental health center. She practically hired me on my first interview. I started working there two weeks before my resignation was final with the abused women's center. I worked there for six and a half years from March 2004 to August 2010.

I had to be hospitalized at a local psychiatric hospital in August 2007. While I was in there I wrote several journal entries.

August 17, 2007

Tonight, I have mixed emotions. I feel numb and anxious. I want to change my medicine because what I am on is not doing the job. I cannot think sometimes. It has not happened since I came into the hospital. I have not gotten to talk to my doctor today, so I do not know what changes he is going to make. I hope he will make some changes.

Today, I feel kind of lost because I have not gotten to talk to anybody about my feelings. I think I will talk to somebody after Mom and Dad leave tonight. If I were at home, I would call the crisis and information line. But I am paying $100.00 a day for the first five days. After that, I do not have to pay anymore, so basically I am paying $500.00 to be here, so why should I not talk to somebody? I feel like crying, but I cannot. I just do not know what to do. We had three groups today. Yesterday they were better. I found out today that my short term disability will start next week. I will receive most of my pay which is good.

I hope to get Betty and Andrew tonight on mom's cell phone when they come to visit me. Mom and Dad have been very supportive of me since I came in the hospital. Valerie has, also, been very supportive of me. My doctor, also, thinks I made the right decision, but if the doctor does not change my medication then, I am not going to be able to make it on the outside world and I would probably die somehow. I am scared I am going to die. My kids and family would miss me, but everybody would be better off without me. I cannot bring myself to write a good bye letter. Every time I start to write one, I start crying and get teary eyed. I just cannot write one. This has been good though because so far it has kept me from killing myself.

Love,
Nancy

August 18, 2007

Today, has been a harder day because I miss Betty and Andrew. I, also, mourned over Daren. Daren was a guy that I dated for almost a year. He lives in a nearby town and came to my house to see me. We only went to his house three times during the year we dated. All of a sudden, he stopped calling me and refused to answer my calls.

I saw the doctor, and he increased my medicine by 1mg in the morning and 1mg in the evening. I slept through the 10:00 a.m. group this morning. I guess because of the increase in my medicine. Then, I slept until 1:00 p.m. Then, I had lunch. We watched a movie about a guy who tried to kill himself but was unsuccessful. Then, we discussed the movie at 3:00 p.m. It made me sad because I want to die too. That is why I am here in a mental hospital, and not outside. At least I am safe in here.

Next week end, we are going to my sister's home, so I can scrap book. I hope we will go on Friday. I am looking forward to going up there. We are planning on going to visit a place in the northern part of the state. Then, I plan on scrap booking with my sister and her church ladies on Saturday.

This afternoon I was asked to get off the phone because evidently I had been on there 30 minutes. I did not realize I had been on there that long. But I talked with my sister and brother.

Mom and Dad are coming up for a visit. Mom said that she brought me some candy and a drink. I am going to try and call Betty and Andrew while Mom and Dad are here. I cannot tell Betty and Andrew where I am because Mom is afraid Nick probably would not let me see the kids for the weekend if he knew I was in here. Of course, I never told them about me going to the hospital for chest pain in June, and it turned out to be my anxiety. I, also, do not want my coworkers to know where I am. I guess I am afraid of what they might say. I am currently waiting for my packet of papers from work. They said that they would send them by certified mail. I hope they come tomorrow since today is Sunday. I have started journaling again. This is my second day to write. Mom brought my paper and a golf size pencil to use like the ones at the hospital. I guess I am done for now.

Love,
Nancy

August 19, 2007

Today has been an OK day. I have been anxious quite a bit. The tech said she could tell that I was feeling anxious. I am worried about dying and am afraid of dying. I prayed to die, but now I want to live. My voices are telling me that I am a liar, and I am afraid of dying. I talked to my sister and Mom today. I got some coupons for developing pictures, and I thought my sister might be interested because she has 12 rolls of film to be developed.

I, also, talked to Tamie and she said she might come and see me tonight or tomorrow night, if I am still here.

I am hoping that I will get to talk to Betty and Andrew tonight on the phone. One of the nurses said I could use Mom's phone to call the kids. I have not talked with them for four days. At least, I have my picture albums with me and I think I will look at them when I get done journaling.

I am nervous about going home. I hope my doctor keeps me until Tuesday. As of right now, I am still worrying about dying. I am scared about dying. I know I have already discussed this earlier in this entry, but I am still anxious about leaving. I prayed I would get hurt and not have to go back to work. Well, I got my prayers answered except that instead of physically being ill I am mentally ill. I am so stupid and I hate myself. How dare I put God to the test like that? I am evil and a Grinch. I hate myself except that I know I am a good Mom which I know that God has blessed me with two beautiful children. I feel like a liar since I am in the hospital and cannot tell Betty and Andrew because if Nick found out he probably would not let me see the kids, and I could not handle that. I guess I will go for now.

Love,
Nancy

While working, I received training to be an In Our Own Voice presenter where consumers tell their story of recovery. Since that time, I have given somewhere between eight to ten presentations. I even gave a speech at a conference for over 300 people.

In addition to this training, I, also, became certified as a Certified Peer Support Specialist which trained me to provide counseling and to help people with setting rehabilitation goals and achieving them. I took a test and flunked the first time and passed the second time to be a Certified Psychiatric Rehabilitation Practitioner. The first time I took it, I did not study. The second time, I started studying in January before the test was in October. This time I knew I would pass.

As a Psychiatric Rehabilitation Counselor, I helped residents set goals and achieve those goals. I led groups such as art and stress management. I was responsible for writing weekly summaries, and presenting my cases of those residents whom I was their case manager to other staff and management. I became attached to one older gentleman whom I will call Chris. Chris and I sat down and talked almost every day that I worked. I missed him when he eventually had to move into a nursing home because he got to the point that he could not walk. There was a lady whom I will call Belle. Belle could not shower by herself because of some past traumatic experience. I had to go in and sit in the bath room with her. She graduated to where she could go in by herself. Belle moved out on her own and eventually died.

I worked at the center for six and a half years, and all that time I suffered from anxiety in the most horrible way. When I get anxious I cannot talk. I just get paranoid and feel as if people are trying to trick me or get me in trouble. The voices that I hear get really bad. I have this ongoing conversation in my head with my voices. My heart beats fast and I feel as if I am having a heart attack. I have been to the emergency room several times because of these bad feelings. Also, I have been to the emergency room several times for chest pain. I even had some tests run on my heart including a heart catheterization. Everything checked out OK, so now when I have those feelings, I can say to myself that I know

I am not having a heart attack because I have had all these tests, and nothing turned out wrong.

While I was working for the rehab center, I would have these awful panic attacks. They were always worse when I was shift leader. One night, I was shift leader when I had a panic attack. I needed to call the supervisor on call for some reason for which I cannot remember. I gave my co-worker the phone who had to tell the supervisor what the problem was. The next week on August 24, 2010 I asked my supervisor if I could work another shift and she said "No." Then, I asked the director of the program if I could work a third shift and she said "No." However, my supervisor and the supervisor on call called me in to have a talk with me. They said that if I could not guarantee them I would not get anxious any more, then, I would need to look for another job. I left that day, and never went back except to clean out my locker.

While I worked for the mental health agency, I came out of the closet that I, too, suffer from a mental illness of Schizoaffective Disorder. For the first time in my life, I did not have to hide this terrible secret and burden any more.

In September 2010 I made the following entries in my journal.

September 7, 2010

Today, I wonder if my therapist will put down I am ready to go back to work when I do not see myself as ready to go back to work for at least a year. Mom and I filled out my Social Security Disability Income papers, and I mailed them at the post office to go out today at noon. I got my hair cut which feels great. I called the bank and got my loan information for my financial aid request from the hospital. I called Bobbie Joan about the conference for my upcoming speaking engagement. I have decided to do it even though I do not feel very good about having to take off work right now. I am worried there might be someone in the audience who might report to Social Security Disability Income that I am doing well enough to speak there, so why can I not work. I feel like people are watching me. I feel that they are following me wherever I go, and I just really feel anxious. I took all three doses of my Clonazepam which lately I have been able to take two. I am really worried about what Jennifer is going to say about my Short Term Disability papers. What if there are cameras in the house watching my every move? I did clean the kitchen tonight including sweeping and mopping, so at least I have done one good thing for myself. Mom said that she would reimburse me for my hair cut if I cleaned the kitchen. I feel so guilty being such a burden financially to my parents. They are paying my child support which is $451.81 a month. If I killed myself by way of a car accident then, nobody would know except God. But then, I would hurt my kids, and I do not want to do that. Maybe, it is a good idea for Mom and Dad to chauffer me around if I cannot commit to not hurting myself.

I do not need to be hospitalized because I know that in the end God will help me. Although, I feel God wants me to die, or else I would not get these ideas in my head. God, please keep me from killing or injuring myself. Despite the pain of living right now, I really do want to live. I just miss my kids. At least I get to see them this weekend. They have no idea that I have been off work since August 24, 2010. That is something I do not want to tell Nick. I am afraid he will take me back to court and I really do not have the money to do that.

I have an appointment with Rachael September 29, 2010. I think I may need to cancel due to the conference that I will be speaking in late September. I am going to go on with the conference I think I already said that. That's all.

Love,
Nancy

September 14, 2010

Right now, I am feeling really anxious. I do not know why. I read Rachael's notes and they did not seem to reflect what has really been going on over the last few months. I was disappointed because I need a strong case to apply for disability. I have not read my doctor's notes but the staff probably is thinking that I am faking it. The voices are, also, calling me bad names. I wish they would stop.

I am still going to the hospital five days a week. My doctor has not told me how long I will keep going. I really enjoy going and get a lot out of it. I do not know what I will do when I stop going. I really enjoy and get a lot out of the program. Mom has already told me that basically she expects me to get up every morning and not sleep all day. This will be hard to do. I am thinking that I might volunteer at the library a couple of days a week because I could get up at 10:00 and work a few hours. However, I feel like I am being followed in my car, so I cannot volunteer until after I am approved for disability.

I hate having to do nothing all evening. I guess I could scrap book tonight, but I really do not want to do that. I need to go to Hobby Lobby and get a blanket to make Andrew's baby blanket even though he is thirteen years old. I eventually ended up buying a cross stitch blanket and finished it in nine months.

I finally got Betty's done. Yeah! However, I still might stitch her birthday on there if I can figure it out. I could work on my speech for the 27th at the aging conference with Bobbie Joan. I had thought about not going, but I decided to go any ways. I need to do it for my own good and feelings of self-worth since I am not working. It is a relief that I do not have to go back to work for at least two and a half months. Thank You Jesus!

I ran into Barbara today at the YMCA pool. I told her I am applying for Social Security Disability Income and asked her to pray for me to get approved. I am wanting to stop paying Nick child support but Mom and Dad do not want me to stop because Dad says I am court ordered and Mom says Nick might change his mind about letting the kids come up here next summer. However, if I get approved that means I would get my money back. I have agreed to pay Mom and Dad back when I get my back pay. Lord, please let me get approved for my Social Security Disability Income. I am anxious about seeing one of their doctors for an exam of my mental state.

Journaling is helping me to let out my feelings when I am anxious. I feel worried about dying. Because I have prayed to die before, I am afraid God is going to honor that and what I really want is to get better. I miss Betty and Andrew.

In my fantasies, Nick and I get back together and I will be with my children. I know he is married to someone else, but I cannot stop thinking about it. I guess I really do not want to be married. I just want my kids back. God, please let me see my kids more often than I do at the present.

I am starting to see through things. My doctor calls it x-ray vision. My voices are getting worse. I hoped I could stay at 400 mg of my medicine, but I may have to go back to 500mg. I think I will talk to the doctor the next time I see him. Whatever it is, it is disturbing to me. I, also, think people can read my mind. I know it cannot be, but it seems real to me.

I think that on Sunday, I am going to go to church with my brother and his wife because Mom and I can go somewhere to swim and then, to their church which starts at 1:00 p.m. I do not think Dad will care as long as I go somewhere. I worry about pleasing Mom and Dad. Especially right now, since I am depending on them for so much. Mom says I should do one thing and Dad says I should do another about telling Nick. I feel like I owe him an explanation. Lord, please let me get my Short Term Disability soon, so I can have a little money to spend on things I need. Well, I am tired now, and I guess I will go for now.

Love,
Nancy

September 16, 2010

I am writing this prayer in desperation. Right now I want to stay at home, but my urge to die is high. I looked in Dad's closet, and his meds are still there. I know that if I took them I could lay down, go to sleep, and never wake up. But that would hurt my children, family, and friends, and I do not want to do that.

Lord, if You do not want me dead then, why do You allow those intrusive thoughts to enter my mind? I do not understand what I have done wrong to deserve this. I have tried so hard to do what You asked me to do. I do not really want to die. I just want the pain to end. God, my heart literally hurts. I want to see Betty and Andrew. Lord, keep Betty safe as she learns to drive and keep Andrew safe as he plays football.

God, I do not understand what I have done wrong. Please help me, God. I do not want to start a suicide note because I am afraid I will finish it. I am so tormented. I hear people talking about me, and I feel as if I am being followed and on camera. I feel as if people are mad at me. Right now, I am a financial burden on my parents. I do not think that Dad wants me to go on Social Security Disability Income, but I feel like it is the only option I have given the condition I am in with the symptoms of my anxiety. I think Mom may have a better understanding of my need to go on Social Security Disability Income but I can talk to my dad about it. God, please make me feel better. I really do not want to die. I am sorry I have prayed to die. I just want the pain to end. Forgive me, Lord, for all that I have done wrong. I wish I could talk to Mom right now. I hear her coughing, so maybe she is awake.

Love,
Nancy

Later, when Betty went to get her driver's permit, she flunked the eye test. When she went to the eye doctor, he said that she has 20/400 vision and there is nothing that can be done to correct it. If she chose to drive, she could not drive on major highways and could not drive at night. Therefore, Betty elected not to drive, but she has friends that help her get around.

I can always depend on God to get me through the tough times. I had to quit work in August 2010. But I received short time disability for three months. I was able to obtain and utilized my cobra benefits.

On October 29, 2010, I was in a serious head on collision with a van when the driver of the van turned in front of me. Therefore, the accident was not my fault. When I went to the hospital, I was diagnosed with a bruised lung, bruised tail bone, bruises on my torso and leg. Also, my car was totaled. My car got paid off between my car insurance and an insurance I had taken out on my loan. This meant that I did not have a car payment. I had an insurance policy on a personal loan which paid my loan payment every month that I was on disability, and that loan finally got paid off in 2013.

In August 2010, I applied for Social Security Disability Income and was approved in September 2010. My benefits did not start until February 2011. In the mean time I received a settlement from my accident, and I was able to cash in a retirement fund. I continued to pay my cobra benefits of $460.00 a month. When I was finally able to buy a car, my loan payment was $100.00 a month cheaper than the last car loan.

Betty started college in 2011. She made the Dean's Honor List her first semester. Because of the eye problem mentioned earlier, she received some funding for her college education from a government agency, and also, obtained a program for her computer that enlarges the letters. Because Betty cannot see to drive, she lives in the dorm on campus. She loves her freedom and does not go home very often.

I am very pleased with how Betty is doing in school. One semester she observed and interacted with a preschool class. She has been approved to student teach prekindergarten in the fall of her senior year. She is, also, involved in her church's preschool Sunday school class.

Andrew played on the football team two years and is currently playing on the soccer team at his high school where he attends. He makes good grades too. My children are beautiful in the inside and the outside. They are both involved in church. They both have a personal relationship with Christ. Matter of fact their step grandfather baptized them both on the same day at the church where he is a pastor. My dad and I were able to watch them be baptized. Then, Betty and her step sister sang a duet.

When the children were with me, I always tried to provide them with the activities that they would be doing with their father. We began having birthday parties for the kids when Betty was five and Andrew was one. We had a party at the hotel, one at the public pool, and one at a pizza place. We, also, had private parties at the supervisor's house. On one occasion, I invited my friend from the college that I attended, her husband, and their son. The last birthday party for Betty was when she was sixteen years old and her parents threw her a big party with about seventy five people.

Also, when their friends had invited them to an activity, I took them to whatever event that it was. Both of them were involved in soccer games, even when the weather was snowy and very cold, I would take them to the game. For instance, one particular game the weather was so cold and snowy that my parents and I had to buy jackets to keep warm.

CHAPTER NINETEEN

———————— ❧ ————————

After I moved out on my own and started working full time, I had to start paying $451.81 a month for child support. Also. I bought my first car. Then, I had to move back in with my parents. While I lived out on my own, I started calling the crisis line to deal with my emotions. I was lonely and was having to deal with my hallucinations and depression. Pretty soon, the staff at the crisis line knew me by name because my children lived in another state, and I would talk about how much I missed them.

Once, I started living with my mom and my dad, I had someone with whom to talk. This time living with my parents was different. For one thing, I had my own car which meant I could go anywhere I wanted. The second thing was that I had my own television set. Although, I hardly watched it in my room except for nights when I could not sleep. It was the only time I would turn it on. It was nice to have that option. Right now, I do not even have it hooked up. A third thing that had changed was that Mom had quit talking about Nick as much. Do not get me wrong she had plenty to say but it had improved and was tolerable. My mom was kind of a controlling person. I do not want to talk bad about her because she passed away in 2011. My dad has given me the freedom that I needed to grow up. As much as I loved my mom, she hurt me in some ways and held me back by telling me when I could do things and when I could not.

Dad tells me, "I'll see you later!" and does not care when I get my hair cut whereas, Mom tried to tell me when I could get my hair cut and when I could not. Now, it is just my dad and I.

I, also, had a cat named Hope. Hope lived to be about thirteen years old. Towards the end of her life, my dad and I had to give her fluids via an IV. The day came when I had to put her to sleep. I was on my way to take her to the vet when I pulled in front of someone and wrecked my car. Then, two days later I was on my way to get an appraisal to get my car repaired when I pulled in front of another guy because the driver in a semi in the middle lane kept waiving me to cross the lane. Therefore, I pulled in front of another truck. It was definitely not my week. I hated to see what my new insurance rates were going to be. Fortunately, they only went up $20.00 per month.

A choice I made some time ago was to stay out of church. I am not a morning person which may seem like a lousy excuse. I just could not get out of bed in time to go to church, so in 2010, I started going to church with my brother and his wife because their church starts at 1:00 p.m. However, I felt pressured from the church members to receive the Holy Spirit. They seemed to dwell on the Holy Spirit as opposed to salvation and asking Jesus into their heart. The pastor, also, preached on not wearing pants, but instead we had to wear dresses and skirts. He preached on wearing long hair while my hair is pretty short. I felt like a backslider every time I would see someone from church in public. I, also, missed Sunday school that the church did not have, so in 2011, I switched back to the church I had grown up in where my dad was attending. People there wear shorts to church. Now I wear shorts on Wednesday nights, but I think pants and jeans are OK for Sunday mornings.

Before I went back to Sunday school I called the church to find out what Sunday school class I should go in. The lady on the other end of the phone recommended I attend the all-women's class. I asked her what service the class was in because our church has two services. She told me it was during the second service which would work out great because my dad went to second service Sunday school, so I dragged myself out of bed in time for church. Then, when I went to go to Sunday school, I asked the welcome ladies where the class was and they told me it was during first service, so I asked them to recommend a Sunday school class for me that I could visit. One of the ladies suggested I go to a certain class. But when I arrived there, that class was supposed to be for married young adults which I am neither. But it turned out to be a class for all ages single or married.

On my first day, the teacher, Joe, said the next Bible study was going to be on Job. I knew at that time that the class was going to be for me because I struggle like Job only my ailment is Anxiety and hearing voices. But I know God is with me.

In May 2011, my mom had a mammogram that was irregular. Next she had a biopsy. The biopsy showed that she had breast cancer. When she went to the surgeon, he told her she could wait up to a month to have her surgery because the kind of cancer she had was slow growing. My mom told the doctor that she wanted to go to my daughter's high school graduation which was three weeks away, so Mom got to go to Betty's graduation.

Here are some journal entries from that time.

May 3, 2011

Dear God,

Today I am at the arthritis doctor with Mom. I went to the hospital first to see about my account at the hospital. Jennifer said that had been taken care of, and I am good to go. We will see what happens. I am worried about Mom's biopsy tomorrow. I have to get up and take Mom to her appointment. I am worried that I won't be able to get up in time to take her even though that is only happened a few times. So I am not going to worry. Lord, please help me to get up in the morning.

Love,
Nancy

May 9, 2011

Dear God,

God, I am deeply saddened that mom has cancer. She is already in so much pain due to her arthritis. Thank You that she came to church with me yesterday. She did really well and left a few minutes early but did well. God, I know her arm pit is going to hurt and she already has to use her arms to get up out of the chair. Could you please let it be a lumpectomy? God, I do not think it is Mom's time to meet You in Heaven because I need her here on earth. Maybe this will be awake up call for her to come to church either with Dad or me. She called today and got an appointment for tomorrow. God, let me be able to go in with her to the doctor tomorrow at the cancer doctor. Mom said that she is not going to have surgery until after Betty's high school graduation. That is fine with me, but I am scared. I feel sorry for dad because Mom told me that he is scared.

Love,
Nancy

May 11, 2011

Dear God,

Thank You Jesus that mom is not going to die from cancer. I went with her yesterday to the surgeon and he told us that Mom has a slow growing cancer and that she could wait up to a month to have her surgery. She is going to have a lumpectomy. Mom scheduled it for June 8, 2011, which means she can go to Betty's graduation on May 21st with no problem. Thank You God! I am just not ready for Mom to leave this world. I need her and she needs me. God, I count it a privilege to help Mom and Dad, although, I do not all ways feel like it, but I want to help them, and now that I am not working I can help them more.

God, I do not want to get stressed out and anxious, but it seems like my anxiety has just gotten worse. Today, I went and had a full body massage. Lord, please help me to get my cobra insurance extended. I really did not know I only had 60 days to send my request into the company. It is eleven months from the time my cobra ends and my Medicare begins. Lord, keep me safe.

Lord, please watch over me as I get the cist cut off my scalp tomorrow. I worry in the back of my mind about the teacher who died of scalp cancer. Please, do not let them have to shave my head because I am going to Betty's graduation, and I do not want to embarrass her.

Lord, please help me get up early in the morning for Betty's graduation because one time I could not get out of bed. I need to look at it like this out of all the times

117

I have gone down there and it only happened once is pretty good.

Love,
Nancy

Friends and family who know me thought that I would have to be hospitalized after the death of my mom who died June 11, 2011. She had breast cancer removed on June 8, 2011. The week before her surgery she had to have some tests done including a Stress Test and a Heart Catheterization. From the test that she had made, the doctor found some blockages in her arteries. However, the doctors decided to do the breast surgery first because it would not take her as long to heal from that as it would from the heart surgery. After the surgery, the surgeon said that tests showed that he had removed all the cancer and that there were no signs of the cancer in her glands.

Dad told me later that Mom had told him on June 10, 2011, how good she was feeling because on the day before she died they walked in the yard to see the flowers which she loved. When they came back into the house she said, "I feel better now than I have felt in weeks." Dad thinks Mom had a premonition that she was going to die because the week before her death she reminded him that she wanted her nephew to officiate her funeral, and had signed a living will. She had, also, changed an insurance beneficiary policy to him that he did not know she had until he examined a bank statement after she died.

On the morning of her death, about 4:20 a.m. Mom woke Dad and me up saying that she could not breathe. Mom insisted that we not call EMS because she wanted my dad to take her to the hospital. Realizing the seriousness of the situation, Dad told me to call 911 while he was getting dressed which I did. My dad thinks that Mom stopped breathing before the ambulance could get to the house which was only about six or seven minutes away but the hospital records indicated that her heart was still beating when she arrived there. While the EMS was coming, Dad gave Mom CPR, but it did not help. Because she had a living will, EMS could only do so much and told us that she had stopped breathing before they took her to the hospital which is about five minutes away. The doctor said that Mom's death was caused by a blood clot going to her lungs and that the death was sudden and there was not any pain.

Dad called Nick to tell him about mom's death, so he could tell Betty and Andrew. He, also, agreed to bring them to the funeral. His wife said that it was a great blessing when Dad told him that he, his wife, and their five children between the two could stay in our house while they were here because they did not know if they could afford a motel.

I must say that his wife must have had a big influence on him in changing for the better. After the funeral, his family, mom's sister with three sons of which one preached her funeral, and my family gathered on the deck where we sang some gospel songs and reminisced about when they were young.

To this day, I get angry with God sometimes because I had begged God not to take my Mom, but He did anyways. When I talk to my dad about it, he says that because my mom was in so much pain from her arthritis which she had in her shoulders, neck, back, knees, and ankles that she is now in a much happier place. I can just vision Mom in Heaven sitting on her balcony watching the birds and tending to her flowers while drinking her coffee like she used to do here at home.

In February 2012, I went to the ear, nose, and throat doctor about my inability to swallow. He said that he found a cist on my tonsil that needed to be removed, so he scheduled my surgery the first week of March to do a biopsy of my tonsil. The week before my surgery I skipped a dose of medicine on Monday and doubled a dose on Wednesday. Missing that dose and doubling the dose along with having to miss my medicines the day of my surgery combined with the anesthetic sent me into a catatonic stage. I had my surgery on Thursday and by Saturday I could not speak, eat, or walk. I was so bad my dad called EMS to come take me to the hospital. This time, they took me to a regular hospital. While I was there, my brother and his wife came to the hospital.

Two ladies showed up in the Emergency Room to ask me some questions to assess whether or not I needed to go inpatient at a psychiatric hospital. The ladies started asking me questions to which I answered, "Yes," to all of them including do you want to hurt yourself and others.

My brother said to me later that he thought if they had asked me if I had ever flown to the moon I would have said, "Yes." From their assessment, they suggested I go into a psychiatric hospital, so once again, I was put into an ambulance and taken to a psychiatric hospital. Once I arrived there I could not speak. The staff who completed my intake said she could tell that I was not suicidal or homicidal despite what the hospital records showed.

I could not figure out how to make a phone call. I got the number for my dad from the nurse, and I lost it. The nurse who had given me the number was not very nice when I went back to get the number again. However, the other nurse there was nice and got my number for me again. There was a really nice patient who dialed the phone number for me to my dad's phone. I was so glad to hear his voice on the phone.

My brother and his wife came to visit me for the first time since I had been in the hospital. I think that they did not know that I had attempted suicide before on three separate occasions until I went to the Emergency Room.

After my hospitalization, I referred my brother and his wife to the Family to Family class a part of the mental illness organization that consists of ten sessions. Both of them said that they learned a lot from the classes including information about medications. My mom and my dad had already gone through the classes at an earlier time. Since that time in the hospital, my brother has gone to several therapy sessions with me, a nurse visit, and a nurse practitioner visit.

Chapter Twenty

In 2001, I left going to the mental health center when I bought health insurance. I began seeing a psychiatrist at a local hospital's psychiatric center. After I had been going there approximately a year, my therapist left and I started seeing another therapist. Then, that center was closed, and my service providers moved. Therefore, I moved with them. Then, in December 2009, I received a call from the doctor's office saying my appointment had been cancelled and I needed to reschedule. When I went to reschedule, the office told me that my doctor had quit practicing. So that January 2010, I went to see a new psychiatrist who was well known in the community. He prescribed medication for my anxiety, but when it did not work, I called his office to discuss the situation with him. He called me back four days later. When I told him the medicine did not do anything for me, he said that no matter what kind of medicine I was on nothing would help me. After that, I changed doctors to a psychiatrist from the hospital in his private office. After my first visit with the doctor, he put me on an anti-anxiety medication for anxiety.

Later, I changed to another therapist at his office because my therapist and I had gotten to the point of just shooting the breeze, and not really doing any therapy. My new therapist taught me how to deal with some of my anxiety by counting backwards by seven from one hundred. Until recently that was the only thing I found that worked.

In January 2010, I joined the YMCA. At first I did not go, so I decided to cancel my membership because I was wasting my money by paying my dues and not going. The lady at the front desk encouraged me to try one more time with a staff who could show me what to do. I decided to give it one more shot. I met with one of the staff who gave me lessons on how to work the weight machines. I started out working out 15 minutes. Then, I got involved in water aerobics four to five days a week and worked out in the pool. I could not go to the groups because I became too anxious. But I did go in the afternoon. Working out makes me relaxed especially since there is usually just one or two other people with me. I prayed that God would give me a place where I could go and not feel anxious. I believe that this is the place. I now work out one hour and forty five minutes.

In May 2011, I decided to try volunteering. At the time I signed up to volunteer, I had to go to an orientation. After the orientation, I had to have a one on one interview with the Volunteer Coordinator. I never heard back, so I assumed I did not pass. A friend of mine from the YMCA who volunteers at that hospital asked me how it was going and I told her that I had never been called to come in to volunteer, so she put in a good word for me with the Volunteer Coordinator. She called about asking me if I were still interested in volunteering and I said "Yes." I told her I was still interested. Then, she asked me to work in the gift shop at another hospital and I agreed to give it a try. The first lady I worked with was really nice. She liked to talk a great deal. On the days she was not there, I would panic. One day after she quit, I had to work by myself, and I had a panic attack. I closed the shop early and called my dad to come help me count the cash register drawer. What normally takes fifteen minutes took me an hour, so back to the drawing board. The lady in charge called and asked me if I would be willing to work the front desk which entailed giving directions in the hospital. However, it was a small hospital. When I started going to day treatment, I had to quit that job.

The supervisor found another job for me at a much larger hospital. This required a lot of interaction with the computer and giving directions to the various places in the hospital. The first night I worked on my own I did OK. The second night I worked by myself I had a panic attack. I told one other staff that I was having a panic attack. The supervisor came out and I went home. I never went back. The lady said she would try and find me another job but it has been several months and I have yet to hear from her. In April 2014, I went back to volunteering at the front desk at the first hospital where I had volunteered at the gift shop.

In September 2011, my vision became very blurry. I went to the eye doctor and he referred me to a specialist in cataract surgery. When I went, I was diagnosed with cataracts in both eyes. The doctor scheduled me for cataract surgery on my eyes one week apart. The cost was $1900.00 that I had to pay up front. When I went for my surgery, the doctor told me that I was his pediatric patient of the day because I was only 42 years old. Following the surgeries, my dad had to put eye drops in my eyes for three weeks. After my surgeries, I started having double vision. My regular eye doctor sent me to another specialist who added a prism to my eye glasses. That seemed to take care of the problem. Before my eye surgery, I could not see two inches in front of my face without my glasses. Now, I can watch TV without my glasses.

During the year of 2011, I signed up to go to Gatlinburg, Tennessee with my sister's church ladies where I had a really good time. I only got anxious a few times while I was gone. We went shopping and to the scrap booking store that had half off of everything in one of the stores. I love that place. I guess it is because I love to scrap book. I have been doing it for at least sixteen years. For my daughter's sixteenth birthday party, I made her a scrap book. Her friends enjoyed looking at it at her party.

My Medicare did not start until February 2013, which was two years after my Social Security started. I did not know it at the time, but I was supposed to have contacted my cobra policy which is only good for eighteen months in order to extend it. Because I missed the window period to sign up again for it, I lost my Cobra in June 2012. After I lost my Cobra insurance, the only choices I had were to either go without insurance or pray for the best luck or get another state policy that was over $600.00 a month which was above my income level. So I elected to go without insurance.

The day I became eligible to go to the mental health center I made an appointment to get services there. The health center did not service private insured clients, and my payment was according to my income. I was able to stay at the mental health center when I got on Medicare. Also, I had to apply for drug coverage once I started Medicare. I was able to get my medications for free before I went on Medicare because I qualified for the patient assistance program.

After getting on Medicare, I pay $450.00 per month for my medicine. For a while, I went to three groups a week, one on Self Esteem, one on anxiety, and one on grief.

Once, I started on Medicare I no longer qualified for groups. This saddened me because I felt like I needed group and some kind of therapy. The only bad thing is that the nurse practitioner told me I needed therapy to help with my anxiety. Unfortunately, I was not allowed to go to therapy except in an emergency. So what was I supposed to do? I had been approved for four therapy sessions to which I used. The only problem I had was that the mental health center does not prescribe my anxiety medicine because it can be addictive. The plan was to slowly take me off of it and put me on another one. In the process I began falling again because my medicine was changed.

I continued to get anxious and have panic attacks every day for almost a year. The medicine that was prescribed for me did not do the job. On several occasions, I asked the nurse practitioner to either increase the medicine or try me on another one, but she refused to change it. After I began to receive Medicare, I decided to change back to the psychiatrist who had prescribed the other medicine since that one worked so well. My former doctor changed my medication to a medicine that improved my anxiety for a little while.

For about six months after I could return to driving from my broken ankle, I could only drive maybe once a week because of my anxiety. On two occasions, I had to have my dad come rescue me because I was too anxious to drive home. When I am anxious, I cannot think or speak and that scares me.

Sometimes, I hear three voices in my head at the same time. I cannot distinguish between God, Satan, and my own thoughts. This really bothers me. I have been on this new anti-anxiety medicine for about two and a half months. I am unable to drive most days, and driving is a precious thing.

On August 26, 2012, I met with my brother, his wife, and my dad about going to the hospital because my medications were messed up; and I was getting catatonic again. After discussing the situation, I seemed to be improving and it was decided for me to wait until the next morning to take me to the hospital. On my way to the kitchen my knees gave out and I fell on my ankle. It was very obvious that it was broken. My sister-in-law called EMS because in order to get to the drive way one had to go down about eleven steps. After waiting two hours and two more calls to the EMS my brother went to the fire station to have them come and help get me down he steps. Just a few minutes after the firemen came to my house, the EMS people came. The technicians said that there had been a triathlon down town, and all of the ambulances were in use transporting runners to the hospital. The EMS had special equipment that they used to negotiate down the steps.

I went to the Emergency Room where I was told that because of my having no insurance if I paid one hundred and some odd dollars the rest of the Emergency fees would be waived. Therefore, my dad paid the amount for me.

I was admitted to the hospital because I had to have surgery on my ankle. My accident occurred on Sunday. Then, on Monday my ankle was too swollen to do the surgery, so it was performed two days after my fall. I had a plate and seven screws put in my ankle.

After my surgery, I had a hard time waking up. When I was taken to my room, the evening meal was being served. The nurse in charge of the unit was at one end of the tray table, and my dad was at the other end closest to my face helping to feed me when I had a seizure. My dad said that this scared him because he was in the room and began to think that I was going through some of the things that Mom went through when she died. He said that it was a bad seizure. Also, he said that the room filled with hospital medical staff when it happened. I was kept in the hospital until Thursday. Then, physical therapy came by and assessed that I needed a walker and a wheel chair because I could not put any weight on my foot. I had to hop with the walker. Also, the wheel chair was very cumbersome to manipulate getting it in and out of the car.

At first, I had a soft cast on my ankle, and I fell several times at home. One time I fell and could not get up by myself even with the help of my dad. Therefore, my dad had my neighbor boys to come and help me get back on my feet. Also, I slept in the recliner, a lift chair, when I came home. I was miserable. Thank God, I only had to take just a couple of pain pills until I started on aspirin.

My second cast that I had on was a hard cast. Again, I could not put pressure on my ankle. Finally, after four weeks in that cast I got to wear a boot. I could not drive because of my broken ankle, and my dad had to chauffer me everywhere I went.

The first day that I used my wheel chair, my dad said that he was not going to do that very often because taking the legs support off and putting them back on was very difficult at first. After several weeks in the wheel chair, dad and I tried using the wheel chair without the legs supports, and that worked much better. After that, we did not use the supports again and eventually dad got used to manipulating the wheel chair in and out of the trunk of the car. Since the accident, my dad has had to drive me to almost everywhere I have to go.

I was supposed to get the boot off in November and the doctor had told me to bring my regular shoe the next time I went in. Unfortunately, that appointment was cancelled and moved three weeks until December 4, 2012, when the boot finally was removed.

My hospital bill was $65,000.00 for five days. That did not include all of the doctor bills. I even received a bill from a psychiatrist that I do not remember meeting. My dad said the psychiatrist came to see me in the early morning and that is why I don't remember. I do not remember very much of the hospital stay at all. I know that two of my friends came and visited me.

My case manager referred me to a program called Spend Down which qualified me for Medicaid for a certain length of time two months in my case. I had already paid some of my bills off, and set payment plans up with others. I applied for the medical facilities to rebill me after I called and gave them my Medicaid information. All of my bills were paid except for $50.00 of the hospital bill. I actually was reimbursed for the bills that I had paid.

Incidentally, while Andrew was playing in his first football game in high school, he sprained his ankle on August 27, 2012, which was the day after I broke my ankle. He was not able to play the rest of the season. However, he made the varsity soccer team at his high school and has gotten to play at those games.

November 2012

Dear God,

I want to talk to Dad, but I am feeling bad and would rather be feeling better before I talk to him. God, please help me to feel like living. I am really anxious. Please take away my anxiousness. I cannot decide if I want to live or die. I think I want to live. Lord, give me a strong desire to live. Take these feelings away. I am going to go now.

Love,
Nancy

CHAPTER TWENTY ONE

─────────────── ∞ ───────────────

I was scheduled to go see my children on the weekend of August 30, 2012. Unfortunately, I did not make it until October 19, 2012.

That was the longest time to go without seeing Betty and Andrew. I had wanted to wait to go until I did not have to wear the cast for my ankle. Dad and I drove straight through on Thursday which turned out to be a tiresome trip. I was terribly anxious when we picked up Betty and Andrew Friday morning at 10:00. I had the kids pictures made at a national chain store. I got so anxious I told the photographer that I did not feel well and needed to come back the next day to select the pictures. However, I did not go the next day. Instead, I went on line and picked them out after I got home. What would have cost me $4.00 a sheet in store cost me $14.00 a sheet on line.

I believe that is the first time that I have left a situation like that. I was miserable practically the whole weekend because of my anxiety. I had to take my anxiety medicine all three days. I felt so guilty not being able to enjoy my children like I should have after not seeing them for four months.

When we returned Betty and Andrew to their home at the end of the Christmas break in 2009, my brother asked Nick if my brother would come and pick up the children then, bring them back home would Nick permit them to come to my home for their week with me in the summer. I don't know when Nick agreed to let them do that because I did not know about it until Mom and I were there in March of 2010.

In July of 2010, my brother drove to their home and brought the children to my house to spend their vacation with me. That was the first time that Andrew, who was 13 years old, had been to his mom's home.

They really had a great time while they were here. We took the kids to see several visitor sights. One place we went to was some caves. My anxiety level was pretty high when we arrived there. I had sprained my knee the March before and was still having trouble with it. I was not so sure about going on a tour, but my family talked me into taking one of the less strenuous tours. I regretted that I went and swore the next time we go I am sitting on a bench. Furthermore, I am not going on any more cave tours.

We, also, went on a dinner cruise on an old steam paddle boat. After the luncheon Betty and Andrew had a ball dancing on the dance floor. The entire excursion was a great deal of fun for all of us. When time came to return them home, my sister and one of her friends drove them back.

I think that I must interject a thought at this point. I believe that Nick has changed his position and attitude since the divorce, because he has been much more cooperative in letting me have the children come to my home. Also, I believe that he has a greater appreciation for how my family has treated our children in comparison to the way that his second wife's former husband's relationship and treatment of her and her children. I am grateful that we do get along very well at this time. I believe that God has intervened on the behalf of my situation.

The second summer my children came to my home was in 2011. Mom had passed away by then, so it was a little difficult.

This time we flew them up in time to go to our family reunion on my dad's side of the family. Betty and Andrew were able to meet some of their cousins, aunts, and uncles. Again, we went on the dinner cruise. They had a DJ there and Betty danced until she got too tired to dance anymore.

We went to see my cousin and her husband who were both in the same hospital room, my cousin for diabetes and her husband for cancer. We left them that day knowing we would never see my cousin's husband alive again. He died in September 2011 and she died in October 2012.

Betty and Andrew flew up June 1st, 2012 for their summer vacation. While they were here, we went to see the mountains of the Eastern part of the state in which I live. The kids seemed to enjoy that. We went to my sister's house where she has a pond in which Andrew can fish.

Betty and Andrew flew to where I live on December 26, 2012, and went home January 1, 2013. This was their first Christmas where I live and we were all excited. We celebrated Christmas dinner after they arrived. That year we were planning to go to an aquarium but could not go because of snowy weather. We did make it to see the Princess Diana collection with my sister and her grandson. We, also, went to see the historical site of a former president's birthplace.

In the summer of 2013, Betty was able to go to an African nation for a mission trip. She worked with children, which is her love and passion. She had to raise $3,600.00 in order to pay her way. She sent out over 60 letters. Then, I sent out about 10 letters requesting monetarily support. She was able to raise the money. I am very proud of her. She spent three and a half weeks there. While she was visiting me that summer, she was able to give her testimony to my Sunday school class.

The summer of 2013, was the fourth summer Betty and Andrew have come to visit me. They flew up on August 4, 2013, in time to go to another family reunion. We went sightseeing and took Betty and Andrew up to the mountains to see the natural bridge. The kids loved riding the ski lift to the top of the mountain and the scenery of the mountains was beautiful. We, also, rode the dinner cruise for a fourth time which my children seem to enjoy that experience. However, this year the band was not so hot, but Betty still danced right along with the music.

CHAPTER TWENTY TWO

On June 21, 2013, I returned to my original doctor who had prescribed for me a stronger anti-anxiety medicine. Unfortunately, I became suicidal, and I had to be hospitalized at a psychiatric hospital. I was able to continue under the care of my doctor because he works at the hospital, and he has an office off campus. I was inpatient for one week, came home, and I had to go back for six more days.

While I was there, I had a roommate who was psychotic. One night I heard this weird sound. I finally figured out she was urinating on the floor. I guess it was because the bathroom door was locked. The staff finally moved her to another room by herself. She, also, took my clothes which is quite funny because I wear a size 2X which is an extra extra large and she wears about a size 2. However, the clothes were finally returned to me.

When I was finally released, I met the criteria to attend intensive outpatient groups. I would like to say, I feel like a new woman with my decrease in anxiety. I am able to drive like I would like too and I do not have panic attacks as often as I was getting them, but unfortunately I cannot say that.

The new medicine which my doctor prescribed helped a little bit but did not take care of the problem with my anxiety. When I asked my doctor to change my medicine, he put me on a medicine that I had been on before. If my family knew, they would be mad at me. But you know I have to do what I have to do to help with my anxiety.

I have been on it two weeks now and I feel somewhat better. I find I can go longer between doses which is a good sign.

The next week after I met with my doctor, I ended up going into the hospital June 28, 2013, because of my suicidal thinking. After staying a week in the hospital, I came home over the weekend and then, ended up going back to the hospital where I stayed for another week. When I was dismissed, I started in the outpatient program and went there from July 2013 until April 2014. Towards the end, my days were cut back from five days a week to three days a week. This is progress. But at this writing, I am not going to the hospital for therapy.

When I was released from the hospital after I broke my ankle, my brother and his wife decided they needed to maintain my medicine. They had looked at my medicine boxes, and they had been messed up. For almost a year they would faithfully bring my medicine after they got out of church on a Saturday or Sunday night. Every time I got a new prescription I had to report to my brother.

My brother insisted that he meet privately with my therapist to discuss what might happen in the case of when my father can no longer take care of me. She declined to meet without me. However that discussion did happen later. Finally, in December 2013, I met with my therapist, my brother, and my dad to discuss what would happen to me when my dad can no longer take care of me, and I had to live on my own with a very limited income. After the discussion about me being able to take care of myself, a decision was made that I was not doing enough around the house.

After my broken ankle, I got out of the habit of cleaning the house. So I devised a plan and drew up a chart of house hold duties. I now use it on a regular basis. For a constant reminder, it now hangs on the refrigerator door.

The drug the doctor put me on is a drug I was on before I went to the mental health center. My doctor was trying me on an anxiety medicine again. Unfortunately it was making me extremely sleepy. I had been sleeping during group in the morning and on the van on the way to and from the hospital. The first day I started back on it I took a nap and felt great when I woke up. I am hoping it is going to help because right now I am not able to drive like I would like to do. I have driven one time in four months.

Driving is my freedom. I hate that Dad has to drive me everywhere. I love to drive, but because of my anxiety I cannot drive. I love being free to stop at the local convenient store for my soft drinks and water. I, also, like to eat chocolate candy. I, also, like my freedom when I go to the YMCA to stay as long as I want to without waiting on Dad. He is great, and I am thankful for his patience and willingness to drive me where I want to go. But like I said, "I would love to be driving on my own." In addition to my being too anxious to drive, I was too sleepy to drive in the morning.

While attending the day program, I rode a van that picked me up in the morning and brought me back in the afternoon. The van driver I had for a while was really nice. However, he talked a lot. He prayed for us when we were having a rough day. He liked to make me laugh. He made fun of me because I just about froze to death in his van when he would roll down the windows. He called me Icee. One day I asked him if he talked this much at home and he said that he does. The van picked me up around seven in the morning, and I arrived at the hospital at 9:00 a.m. Because I usually slept on my way there, the driver had to wake me up when we arrived at the day treatment center. In the afternoon, I usually spent about an hour and a half returning home.

I really liked going to group. When I arrived there, I bought an omelet with bacon, mushrooms, and shredded cheese. I, also, drank a caffeinated soft drink to try and stay awake. I hated that I kept sleeping in group because I really received a lot out of group. It helped me to listen to my peers and talk about my issues. We spent the first fifty minutes checking in how we were doing at the present. I almost always said, "I am anxious." As the day went by my anxiety decreased. By the time I got home, I was no longer anxious. Thank You Jesus! On the days I did not go to the day program at hospital I felt very anxious because I slept late. I hate that feeling. I stay anxious nearly all day up unto the evening. For whatever the reason, I just cannot get out of bed. I have never been a morning person. That is why I am glad I went to the hospital for Transition Groups because it gave me a reason to get up and get started on the right track. I have discovered that I get up earlier than I used to now that I have gotten used to getting out of the bed earlier.

Dad and I go to the grocery store once a month to trade for the month. The local store has Senior Citizens' Day when they give a discount for being a senior citizen. We actually went to the store and was home by 11:30am.

In the year 2013, Betty and Andrew flew up here for Christmas. Two weeks before Christmas Betty called me to ask me if anyone in our family had stomach issues. I told her that I have GERD and Acid reflux, and that I take medicine for my stomach issues.

Betty explained that she was having stomach issues, and was going to the doctor. When she got home from the doctor's office, she called and said that the doctor had told her that she may have gall bladder issues and might have to have surgery.

The kids were supposed to fly up here on December 26, 2013. Betty called and told me that she had an appointment to have a test scheduled on the 26th at 7:45 a.m. which would not be a problem because their flight was scheduled to leave at 5:00 p.m. However, her dad scheduled a doctor's appointment with the surgeon on December 31st

The kids were scheduled to leave on January 1st. Therefore, Dad had to change the plane tickets. It worked out great for several reasons. First of all, when they were originally scheduled to leave here there was a snow storm in the connecting city and many flights were cancelled in and out of that airport as well as many other airports. Another good thing that happened was that part of the original price was refunded because the ticket was cheaper. Betty and Andrew made it home safely and on time.

Betty went to the surgeon, and he said that she does not have a problem with her gall bladder, so she did not need to have surgery. Instead the doctor tried her on some stomach medicine to see if that helped. It did, and she no longer has to take any medicine.

In August 2013, our church started having a recovery program. This Christian ministry which is a national organization is aimed for people who have hang ups, hurts, and habits. It is designed to have a testimony every other week and a lesson every other week. After the group meets, every one breaks up into small groups like anxiety, depression, substance abuse, and sexual promiscuity. It works the same as A.A. in that participants earn tokens for the time spent in recovery. The program recently changed the format and it is now four hours a week when we will have a meal, large meeting, small groups, and then, Cross Talk Café which is the time that we can socialize. I like this program and have grown in Christ. I am currently involved in a step study of the steps that occur in recovery. I now have an accountability partner whom I call quit often.

The week before my scheduled Spring Break in 2014 with Betty and Andrew I had to be hospitalized. The doctor wanted to do an overhaul on my medications and felt I needed to be in the hospital where he could see me every day. I went in on five medications for my mental illness: two anti-psychotics, two anti-depressants and one anti-anxiety. The doctor did do an overhaul on my medications and I came out with two anti-psychotics and a medicine that treats both depression and anxiety. The doctor, also, prescribed an extra anti-anxiety medicine. I was hospitalized on Tuesday and left on Friday. I remember when I went in I was extremely anxious, and I had to complete a safety plan. It took about thirty minutes because I was confused. Then, when I went to leave, they lost my plan. Later, I remembered signing my copy of the plan with my social worker as I was preparing to leave. By the time I was ready to go, I was anxious and confused. I needed help getting my belongings in a giant paper bag. But I decided it would be best if I did not yell "Help!" down the hall because I was afraid the staff would come running, so I went and asked the staff to help me.

When my dad came and picked me up, I knew he would be upset with me if I were anxious but I could not help it. I told him I was really better than I appeared. Dad told me he did not think it helped any for me to go in patient. By the next day, I was feeling some better and then, I had a really good day on Sunday. Unfortunately, by Thursday night I was experiencing severe anxiety and confusion. I did not even go to the recovery program because I was so miserable. I was not looking forward to a week of anxiety and telling my children that when I am really quiet for long periods of time that I am anxious, but I felt like they deserved to know.

On March 15, 2014, my dad and I picked the kids up at their house for their Spring Break. I had already told my dad that I wanted to discuss my anxiety with Betty and Andrew because my anxiety is so bad. At first, I apologized for my hands shaking very badly. I know they must wonder what is going on. After we picked up the kids on Saturday, we went to the store. While I was there I had a panic attack.

Andrew helped a woman out who was in line to get her groceries onto the checkout counter top. I was proud of him, but could not say anything because of my anxiety. Later, that evening when I felt better, I called in my children and told them about my anxiety being bad. I asked them if they had any questions and they both answered "No."

I prayed to the Lord that I would not be anxious when I picked the kids up and when I took them back and several days in between. God honored my prayer request for picking them up and taking them back. Unfortunately, my anxiety sky rocketed while I was there. Not only was I feeling anxious and shaking all over, but I got confused. I called my dad into a bedroom and told him I thought something was wrong with my medicine. We discussed the situation and decided I needed to call my doctor the next day because it was too late to call him that day which was a Wednesday after 5:00p.m. The next day, I did not take my anxiety medicine and I seemed to get better. Then, I took a dose in the afternoon of my anxiety medicine and I started getting confused again. I called my pharmacist and asked him if the anxiety medicine which I was taking could cause confusion and shaking, and he confirmed that it could. I went off the anxiety medicine, and I have not taken it since. I continue to get anxious. For instance, I got anxious yesterday after noon but was able to lay down for a while. After I had rested, my anxiety left, and I was able to go to my recovery program without any anxiety.

March 22, 2014

Dear God,

Thank You for a good three days. The last two days were pretty good. I had an awful two days on Tuesday and Wednesday. I figured out what was causing me to feel confused and anxious; it was my anxiety medicine. I was miserable Wednesday. I was shaking all over, and I could not focus because I was confused, so on Thursday, I did not take my morning dose of anxiety medicine, and by the afternoon I was feeling much better. Then, I took the afternoon dose and I started feeling confused again. So I called my pharmacist at the drug store and asked him if my anxiety medicine could cause those symptoms of confusion and jerking, and he said, "Yes." Next I called my psychiatrist's office and he said that he would see me at the hospital the next day, but I informed his office that I was out of town and would not be able to see him on Friday. However, I had a scheduled appointment in his office the next Tuesday. Therefore, I had to wait until Tuesday to see him. I planned on going Monday morning and then, pick back up Wednesday because I cannot go to see him in his office and go to the out-patient program on the same day.

Lord, we are going to meet my brother and his wife at a restaurant at 4:30 p.m. Please help me to keep from getting anxious this afternoon and tonight. So far, I have not gotten anxious today. I cleaned out my car. We got home at 12:00 a.m. this morning. I am doing Dad's laundry now. I read three books since last Thursday, and I am going to buy another book this afternoon after we eat at a restaurant. I now fill my days with going to the YMCA, and I volunteer one day a week at the local community medical center. I am in several Bible studies: one on Sunday morning, one on Tuesday night, one on Wednesday night, and one on Thursday night. I am learning to trust in the Lord on a daily basis.

I have not driven in three months, and my goal is to drive again in the next month. Hopefully, by the time this book is published I will be able to drive again.

Love,

Nancy

One more entry from my journal before I close out this book

April 14, 2014

Dear God,

Right now I am at my volunteer job. Please help me not to be anxious. I am going out to supper with Dad after I get off from here. Then, I will go to my recovery classes. I just finished lesson seven in my step study book. It is about picking an accountability partner which I already have. Lord, please help me to be a good accountability partner. Please help me not to be anxious when I go to church tonight for recovery groups. I just got a refill of Coke and bought some gum at the gift shop. It has been a while since I bought gum at the gift shop. I was getting it at the gift shop at the hospital where I was going, but then, I decided to watch my sugar intake. Then, because I was going on Tuesdays, Thursdays and Fridays the gift shop was not open those days.

I do not know if I told you or not but I graduated from the outpatient program last Friday. I was given a one day notice which I do not think was fair.

I had my Social Security Disability Income reviewed by the SSDI people. The lady in charge said that she is getting records from the places where I had received treatment.

They have been sent requests of information from SSDI. I know I cannot work. Some days, I cannot volunteer because my anxiety gets so bad. My hands are still shaking pretty badly. But at least, I am not as confused as I was on Spring Break. Lord, please help my shaking hands to stop shaking.

Thank you Lord,
Nancy

On July 5, 2014, I sold my car back to the dealership where I purchased it. I was not using it, and it just sat in the driveway. It was costing me $400.00 a month. It feels great not having a car payment and an insurance payment. This means that I will have an extra $400.00 to spend which is good because the cost of my medicine went up to $450.00 a month.

I thank God that my car was paid off when I took it back to the dealership. I am going to be able to give Dad some money for food and gas every month. With this income or lack of bills I will be able to give Betty and Andrew more money for their birthdays.

Conclusion

Through all of the pain and suffering that I've endured, God has never left me no matter how lonely I feel. Sometimes I question God, What have I done to deserve this? Then, I think about Job, the Old Testament character, who suffered without sinning. I believe in recovery. My faith in God gets me through every day. I still have my struggles especially with anxiety. It has been my privilege to give my testimonial speech to several organizations including an organization where an international psychiatrist was the key note speaker. Another group was a police organization. The last time I gave my testimony was to my Sunday school class where I attend church.

But through it all, Christ has been there for me. He has carried me when I couldn't walk. He has spoken for me when I couldn't speak for myself. I am definitely not saying that I am Job in the Bible, but through my struggles, I have not given up on God.

Therefore, *Don't tell me I Can't.*

About the Author

———————— ✺ ————————

Nancy Elizabeth Phillips became a born again Christian at the age of twelve. At an early age she started working in the church through different programs such as a mission organization for teenage girls, the bus ministry, and the church orchestra. She graduated from a Baptist University with a Bachelor's degree in Family Therapy. She worked in the mental health field for nine years with six years as a rehabilitation counselor. While working in the program, she earned her Peer Support Specialist Certification, became an In Our Own Voice presenter, and a Certified Psychiatric Rehabilitation Practitioner. Nancy has done presentations about her recovery, and is a published author. She has two children whom she is very proud of their accomplishments. Nancy, also, goes to church where she is in a recovery program. She continues to work on recovery from Anxiety, Depression and Schizoaffective Disorder.

Her dream was to write this book in order to give God the praise He deserves.